Physical Characteristics of the English Springer Spaniel

W9-BRJ-756

(from The Americ... dard)

Body: Short-coupled, strong and compact. The chest is deep, reaching the level of the elbows, with well-developed forechest. The back is straight, strong and essentially level. Hips are nicely-rounded, blending smoothly into the hind legs. The croup slopes gently to the set of the tail.

Tail: Carried horizontally or slightly elevated and displays a characteristic lively, merry action, particularly when the dog is on game.

Hindquarters: Thighs are broad and muscular. Stifle joints are strong. Hock joints are somewhat rounded, not small and sharp in contour. Rear pasterns are short and strong, with good bone. Feet are the same as in front, except that they are smaller and often more compact.

Coat:. On the body, the outer coat is of medium length, flat or wavy, and is easily distinguishable from the undercoat, which is short, soft and dense.

Color: (1) Black or liver with white markings or predominantly white with black or liver markings; (2) Blue or liver roan; (3) Tricolor: black and white or liver and white with tan markings, usually found on eyebrows, cheeks, inside of ears and under the tail.

Size: Ideal height at the shoulder for dogs is 20 inches; for bitches, it is 19 inches.

English Springer Spaniel

by Haja van Wessem

Contents

Photography by Carol Ann Johnson and Haja van Wessem, with additional photographs by:

Norvia Behling, Carolina Biological Supply, Karin Brostam, Mrs. A. Corbett, Doskocil, Isabelle Francais, James Hayden-Yoav, James R. Hayden, RBP, Bill Jonas, Dwight R. Kuhn, Dr. Dennis Kunkel, Mikki Pet Products, Phototake, A. H. de Raad, Jean Claude Revy, Dr. Andrew Spielman, Karen Taylor and C. James Webb.

Illustrations by Renée Low

Special thanks to Evelyn & Tyce W. Beede and Sylvie Linossier, and all owners of dogs featured in this book.

KENNEL CLUB BOOKS: ENGLISH SPRINGER SPANIEL
ISBN: 1-59378-227-6

Copyright © 1999 • **Revised American Edition: Copyright © 2003**
Kennel Club Books, Inc., 308 Main Street, Allenhurst, NJ 07711 USA
Cover Design Patented: US 6,435,559 B2 • Printed in South Korea

History of the
ENGLISH SPRINGER SPANIEL

EARLY SPANIEL HISTORY

Spaniels can be considered among the oldest dogs in history. Their origins go back a very long time. It is very likely that the spaniel got his name from the countries surrounding the Mediterranean where he lived, "namely" Spain. He might also have gotten his name from the Basque word *Espana* or from the several spaniel-like breeds in France that are called *épagneuls*. The name spaniel might also be derived from the French *s'espagner*, which means to crouch.

Proof of the antiquity of the breed can be seen in the first mention of a spaniel in Irish Laws in A.D. 17 in a statement that water spaniels had been given as a tribute to the King. Spaniels also traveled to Wales where they were the treasured dogs of King Howell Dha (Howell the Good). The King's love for his spaniels went as far as giving them a special mention in one of the country's laws in A.D. 94: for the price of one spaniel, one could buy a number of goats, women, slaves or geese!

From its ancient beginnings, the English Springer Spaniel has evolved into one of the most well-rounded dog breeds—working dog, champion in all areas of the dog sport and, of course, a favorite among pet owners.

A working Springer Spaniel from Holland, where the breed is very popular.

In these laws a division of the mammals was made into birds, beasts and dogs. The dogs were subdivided into trackers, greyhounds and spaniels.

The first mention of a spaniel in English literature comes as early as Geoffrey Chaucer (1340–1400) and Gaston de Foix, who died in 1391. Chaucer, the poet of *The Canterbury Tales,* refers to the spaniel several times (e.g., "for as a Spaynel she wol on him lepe"), which proves that the spaniel was known in England 600 years ago. Gaston de Foix mentions the spaniel in his work

9

English Springer Spaniel

Miroir de Phoebus or, as it is also known, *Livre de Chasse*. Gaston de Foix, a feudal baron who lived in France near the Spanish border, was convinced that Spain was the country of origin of the spaniel. "Another manner of hound there is, called hounds for the hawk, and Spaniels, for their kind came from Spain, notwithstanding that there be many in other countries. Such hounds have many good customs and evil. Also a fair hound for the hawk should have a great head, a great body, and be of fair hue, white or tawny (i.e., pied, speckled, or mottled), for they be fairest and of such hue they be commonly the best." He then describes them as being "hounds (the word dog was then not used) with a great head and a great, strong body. Their color is red and white of orange roan, but black and white can also be seen. They run and wag their tail and raise or start fowl and wild beasts. Their right craft is the partridge and the quail. They can also be taught to take partridge and quail with the net and they love to swim."

The Springer Spaniel likely derived from hunting dogs on the Continent, where they remain popular today.

The English Water Spaniel, predecessor of the English Springer Spaniel, as illustrated by P. Reinagle, R.A., in *The Sportsman's Cabinet*, 1803.

Another early reference to *spanyellys* occurs in the *Boke of St. Albans* (1486), also named *The Book of Field Sports*, written by Dame Juliana Berners, prioress of Sopwell Nunnery, Hertfordshire. It is obviously a school book and it is assumed that the book was written for the use of King Henry IV's son, Prince Henry, to teach him to read and make him acquainted with the names of the animals and phrases used in venery and field sports. In the book there is frequent mention of spaniels in the royal household. Thus we read that "Robin, the King's Majesty's Spaniel Keeper" was paid a certain sum for "hair cloth to rub the Spaniels with."

THE FIRST SPRINGERS

We find the first mention of springer spaniels in the book *Treatise of Englishe Dogges* (1570) by the famed dog scholar Dr. Caius (pseudonym for John Keyes). Dr. Caius described the way the dogs were taught to let themselves be caught under the net and classified all sporting dogs under two headings: *Venatici*, used for the purpose of hunting beasts, and *Auscupatorii*, used for the hunting of fowl. He subdivided this latter group into land spaniels and "Spaniells which findeth game on the water." He named this group *Hispaniolus*. He also was of the opinion that these dogs originated in Spain. He describes them as white with red markings or the rarer solid red or black. The land spaniels were praised for their work of springing game for the hounds and the hawks to chase.

In the days of Henry VIII the many royal banquets required a lot of food, and game was an important part. Game such as partridges, quail and pheasant, rabbits and hares were caught in snares but because of the never-ending demand, a more speedy method of catching the game was needed. This method was found in "netting." Spaniels were used to drive the birds towards the fowlers who stood ready with their extended nets. Dog and bird were caught under the net. The spaniels that were used for this kind of work were called sitting or setting spaniels, and they are the ancestors of our modern setters.

With the invention of the gun, netting disappeared and game was caught by shooting. The setting spaniels were used to find the game and point it, and the spring-ing spaniel flushed the game from the cover so that it could be shot.

In the *Sportsman's Cabinet*, written by Nicolas Cox and published in 1803, we find this description of the spaniel: "The race of dogs passing under the denomination of spaniels are of two kinds, one of which is consid-erably larger than the other, and are known by the appellation of

No gundog can be a champion without proving his working ability. Illustrated here is the English Springer Spaniel Club at a 1925 field trial at Wootton, near Bedford.

the springing spaniel—as applicable to every kind of game in every country: the smaller is called the cocker or cocking spaniel, as being more adapted to covert and woodcock shooting, to which they are more particularly appropriated and by nature seem designed." We may assume, therefore, that the Cocker Spaniel derives his name from the woodcock or—as some believe—the cockpheasant.

In the 16th and 17th century, another group of spaniels was recognized: the toy spaniels. Since the toy spaniel in those days was bigger and heavier in build than our modern toy spaniels, it is very likely that there was a relationship among the Blenheim Spaniel, the King Charles Spaniel (English Toy Spaniel) and the hunting spaniels. Moreover, it wasn't unusual for Blenheim Spaniels to be used in the field.

In the 18th century, the term springing spaniel was gaining ground as a description, not of a

Rufton Repeater, owned by J. A. Wenger, was considered an excellent specimen of the breed in the 1920s.

particular variety but of the group of gundogs that sprung their game. All land spaniels came under this heading and the varieties we now know as Clumber, Welsh and English Springer, Field, Cocker and Sussex Spaniel were all springing spaniels.

In the beginning of the 1800s, the Boughey family of Aqualate in Shropshire developed a distinct strain of spaniel that they bred very carefully and for which they kept a stud book for over a

A working English Springer Spaniel swiftly and eagerly runs to his master to deliver the booty (in this case, a rabbit).

It is likely that the English Toy Spaniel, considered one of the toy spaniels, is related to the hunting spaniels.

century. After 100 years of selective breeding, an English Springer Spaniel was born in 1903 that was to become famous as Field Trial Champion Velox Powder, owned by C. Eversfield of Denne Springers. Velox Powder traces back to Mop I, the first dog to appear in the Aqualate register in 1812. The Boughey family kept their interest in English Springers until the 1930s.

In the late 1800s, there was a great interest for Springer Spaniels because of their outstanding working abilities. The Sandringham Kennels of King Edward VII in Norfolk contained many fine Springers that were known for some time as Norfolk Spaniels. Not only in Norfolk but also in other parts of England, all parti-colored spaniels were known as Norfolk Spaniels until after 1900 when they all became Springer Spaniels.

In those early days Springer Spaniel breeders used other breeds to fix the English Springer Spaniel type. In the very early 1900s, Mr. Phillips bred a Cocker Spaniel bitch to an English Springer to produce the winning

The English Cocker Spaniel was classified as a cocking spaniel.

Springer Eng. Ch. Rivington Sam. Breeders have also made use of English Setters, Pointers and even a Clumber to improve the bone on the dogs. The story goes that Field Spaniels have been used to improve the English Springer's heads. Orange-colored puppies from a litter with an English Setter were registered as Welsh Springers. A daughter of the famous Beechgrove Will was registered as a Field Spaniel.

In 1885 the Spaniel Club was founded. The first field trial was held in 1899 on Mr. William Arkwright's estate in Derbyshire. Mr. James Farrow and Mr. C. A. Phillips were the judges. However, it was not English Springer Spaniel but a Clumber Spaniel, Beechgrove Bee, owned by Mr. F. Winton Smith, who won. A year later it was an English Springer Spaniel by the name of Tring who took the top honors.

In 1902, The Kennel Club recognized the English Springer Spaniel as a specific variety of

spaniel and the Spaniel Club drew up the standard for the breed and submitted it to The Kennel Club for approval. It was not long before the first Springers became bench champions. Beechgrove Will of Mr. Winton Smith was the first dog to become a champion and Major Harry Jones's Fansom was the first bitch to do so. The first English Springer to become Field Trial

The Clumber Spaniel was used in early breeding programs to improve the Springer's bone.

Champion, in 1913, was Rivington Sam, out of the Cocker bitch Rivington Ribbon and by Spot of Hagley. Sam was the grandsire of Field Trial Champion Rex of Avendale, who features in the pedigrees of many of our modern English Springers.

In 1921, the English Springer Spaniel Club was founded and the breed enjoyed increasing popularity. The early pioneers held strongly to the view that the English Springer was basically a working dog and their aim was to

breed for working abilities as well as breed conformation.

Many famous breeders and affixes from those early days can be remembered, such as Mr. Winton Smith (Beechgrove); Mr. H. S. Lloyd (Of Ware); the Duke of Hamilton (Avendale); Mr. C. A. Phillips (Rivington); Mr. C. C. Eversfield (Denne) and Lady Portal (Laverstoke).

The Welsh Springer Spaniel is a close relative of the English Springer.

HISTORY OF THE BREED IN GREAT BRITAIN

Until 1920 the fanciers of the breed were not much interested in

The Sussex Spaniel is another of the springing spaniels.

Ware and Eng. Ch. Denne Duke. Mr. C. A. Phillips's Rivington dogs were a strong force for a considerable period of time. As late as 1951, Rivington Glensaugh Glean won the Spaniel Championships. His name appears in many pedigrees and he has sired at least eight field trial champions.

Notable breeders in the years between the two wars were: Hon. George Scott (Marmion), Mr. R. Grierson (of Solway), Miss Morland Hooper (Ranscombe) and Mr. H. S. Lloyd (the internationally famous "Wizard of Ware") who was world famous not only for his Cockers but also for his Springers. Eng. Ch. Springbok, Eng. Ch. Jambok and Eng. Ch. Jamson of Ware were well-known winners and sires. Eng. Ch. Springbok of Ware eventually went to the States.

As with so many breeds and clubs, World War II put an end to all activities. Shows and breeding were restarted after the war, but it took some time before the breed-

A beautiful head study of Foxfield Alpha, owned by R. Bowden. This dog was a huge winner, including Challenge Certificates, in 1932 and 1933.

Regalia, owned by Miss Morland Hooper, retrieves a moorhen. The dog holds the bird very lightly and is very serious about its work.

showing. They worked their Springers and the only breeders who used to show their Springers were Mr. W. Arkwright and Mr. F. Winton Smith.

Still, the breed did well because the Springer was not only a much loved pet but was also very helpful in bringing in rabbit, which was a very important food for many country families between the two wars.

Notable stud dogs in the first two decades of the century were: Eng. Ch. Velox Powder, Eng. Ch. Rivington Sam, Eng. Ch. Rex of Avendale, Eng. Ch. Flint of Avendale, Eng. Ch. Springbok of

ers had attained the pre-war level of quality.

Although not often shown, Boxer of Bramhope, owned by Mrs. Mary Scott, had a tremendous influence on the breed as a sire; and he features in almost every pedigree. The Bramhope Kennels produced a great number of winners and famous sons of Boxer are Eng. Ch. Alexander of Stubham, Eng. Ch. Peter of Lortonfell and Eng. Ch. Studley Major.

New breeders after the war were Joe Braddon (of Ide) and Andrew and Jimmy Wylie (Pinehawk). The Wylie brothers produced many field trial winners.

In the 1950s, The Kennel

Eng. Ch. Banchory Boy, belonging to the Countess of Howe, offering a retrieved rabbit. Circa 1934.

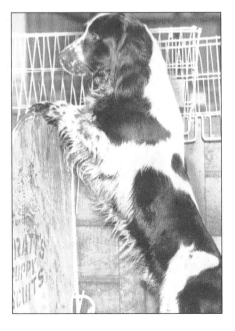

Club decided to change the rules for winning the title of champion. Until then a dog could only become a champion if he had won three Challenge Certificates (CCs) and a qualifier in the field. In the '50s The Kennel Club decided to introduce the title of Show Champion for a dog that had won three CCs and Champion for the dog that had won three CCs and had also qualified in the field. A Dual Champion is a dog that has obtained the title of Show Champion and Field Trial Champion as well. The number of Springers that have become Dual Champions is few. Among them are Horsford Hetman and his son Thoughtful of Harting as

"Lonely?" That was the caption for Sidbrook Ranger, owned by Mr Hebstrip. This photo was taken by Keystone at the 1937 Crufts Dog Show.

17

A Spaniel painting by Reinagle, circa 1830, shows a Springer Spaniel after having flushed the ducks.

well as Flint of Avendale, who later went to Canada.

The first dogs to win the new title of Show Champion were Bonaventura of Bramhope, Stokeley Sea Sprite and Sandylands Susanna. Mrs. Hanna

Stokeley was especially in favor of mixing show and working lines. In 1958, Eng. Ch. Stokeley Higham Tona was the dam of two field trial winners, Rogue and Scamp, who later went to Italy to Mr. Marco Valcarenghi and became Italian champions. In order to do so they had to win four CCs at shows as well as qualify in the field.

Alexander of Stubham, owned by Mrs. F. Oughtred Till, won 22 CCs, which was a record for those days, and he joined his sire Boxer of Bramhope as one of the leading stud dogs in the breed.

In the '60s and '70s, competition was very strong and very few new faces were seen in the

English Springer Spaniels excel at both field and water work.

ring. One of the kennels that dominated the ring was Hawkhill, owned by Judith Hancock. In partnership with Jimmy Cudworth, Judith steered Hawkhill Connaught to a position no English Springer had attained before. He was a top dog in 1972 and 1973. He won over 50 CCs and some 16 Groups. St. Pauli Girl of Moorcliff and Prince Consort of Moorcliff were bred by Hawkhill and owned by Ernest Froggat, who bred winners

A 1928 painting by Reinagle of what appears to be an ancestor of the Springer Spaniel.

himself including Eng. Sh. Ch. Moorcliff Dougal and Eng. Sh. Ch. Moorcliff Gamecock, who was the sire of the famous Connaught.

On the working side, a famous dog is undoubtedly Hales Smut, owned by Arthur Cooke and bred by Mr. Keith Erlandson. He sired at least 13 field trial champions. Mr. Erlandson's prefix Gwibernant is well known all over Europe.

Other breeders who certainly deserve a mention are Mrs. O. Hampton (Larkstoke), Mrs. E. Dobson (Tyneview), Mr. and Mrs. D. Miller (Feorlig), Mrs. J. Taylor (Cleavehill), Mr. C. Muirhead (Shipden) and Mr. and Mrs. Woodward (Wadeson).

The dog that caused a pleasant stir was certainly Eng. Sh. Ch. Elimvek Earthbound, who was still a youngster when he won the Gundog Group at the Crufts Dog Show in 1998. He was the top-winning English Springer Spaniel

Mompesson Remember Me is the breed record holder in Great Britain with 54 CCs, as well as a qualifier in the field. He is bred and owned by Mrs. F. Jackson.

Eng. Ch. Dry Toast was a huge winner in the UK during the early 1930s.

Eng. Sh. Ch. Hawkshill Connaught was Top Dog in 1972 and 1973, and the winner of 50 CCs.

January 1889, chestnut brown and white, very likely a British import and considering his color, an English Springer.

A while passed before the next registration, but in 1902 one can find the registration of a litter of Cocker Spaniels of which several later were shown as Springers. Their sire was Rivington Red Coat and their dam Colwyn Rose. Colwyn was

Int. Ch. Springbok of Ware went to the United States, where he also became a champion.

of 1998, closely followed by Eng. Sh. Ch. Wadeson Inspector Wexford, another Group and Best in Show winner.

Although the aim of the club has always been to support field and show, it was unavoidable that a distinct working-type English Springer Spaniel came into being. There is a tendency in working lines to breed for a smaller and lighter dog whereas the show Springer is heavier in bone and larger. Unfortunately, both the show and working enthusiasts have adopted breeding plans to suit their goals best, be it showing or working, and the difference in type has become such that they have almost made the English Springer into two separate breeds.

THE SPRINGER ON THE CONTINENT

The first spaniel to be registered in the Dutch stud book (number 123) was Wallace, born in

the prefix of Mr. Porter in England and several Colwyns have Breasides in their pedigree, both being the prefixes of breeders of Cockers and Springers. We may therefore safely assume that interbreeding between Cockers and Springers took place and that depending on their size the offspring was registered as Cockers, Fields or Springers and maybe even, depending on their color, as Welsh Springer Spaniels.

In 1925, when the English Springer was surviving but not

really thriving, an English Springer by the name of Hick was born. His dam was Shalassa (Ranger of Ranscombe x Grass Bessie) and his sire Cassio Trooper (Ch. Flint of Avendale x Cassion Nixie). Hick was a tri-colored dog, bred by Mrs. A. Pike and owned by Mrs. L. van Herwaarden, who with her husband had started in Cocker Spaniels (Wagtail). Hick won

F. Warner Hill's Eng. Ch. Beauchief Benefactor was an outstanding Springer of the 1930s.

many championship awards in Holland, Germany and Belgium and proved himself in the field as well.

After the war in 1947, a dog and a bitch were imported: Horsford Hence and Horsford Tara. Their owner, Mr. J. G. Sillem, took the suffix Van het Watervliet and bred his first litter with these two in 1948. He bred them again in 1951.

An important import was Winch Crocidolite (Rollicker of Ranscombe x Winch Brown Jewel), born in 1953, bred by Mrs. G. G. Crawford and owned in Holland by Mr. T. Plate. In 1956 Winch Crocidolite sired a litter for Mr. Cremer out of the bitch Wilby Stokedoyle Tina. This was the start of the Van Duin en Kruidberg Kennels that was so successful in later years. Mr. Cremer, later in partnership with Mr. and Mrs. Kingma, built a line of work and show Springers and many champions had the Duin en Kruidberg suffix.

In 1965 Mr. G. Radsma bred his first Van de Springershoek

The top-winning stud dog of 1985 was Eng. Sh. Ch. Chaigmarsh Sudden Impact. His sire, Ardencote Alexander, was also a top-winning stud dog, as well as his offspring, Mompesson Dream Chaser.

Dutch Ch. Hick was the dominating Springer in Holland in the 1920s.

litter. In this litter a puppy was born that was to become very famous as a show dog and sire: Mizar van de Springershoek. He became a champion in 1968, the second Springer to do so. His litter sister Sagitta van de

Springershoek followed suit a year later.

In 1970 Mr. and Mrs. Viergever, who as the owners of Ch. Mizar van de Springershoek were well into Springers by now, imported a bitch from Britain by the name of Larkstoke Sarcelle, bred by Mrs. O. Hampton, out of Eng. Ch. Larkstoke Ptarmigan and by Eng. Ch. Teesview Tarmac. She had the beauty of her parents and she passed on their working ability to her offspring. Sarcelle was the first English Springer to win a Best in Show in Holland at an international all-breed championship show.

By this time the difference in type between working and show Springers became apparent in Holland as in Britain, and the working Springers gained more and more in popularity. The gap between the two types has continued to widen to such an extent that nowadays we seem to have reached a point of no return.

In addition to Mr. Cremer and his Van Duen en Kruidberg kennel, another important breeder of the show Springers was the Dongemond kennel founded by Mr. and Mrs. Arendse, which produced many show champions. In the early '80s Mr. de Vette imported Saxdalens Dette de Vette from Denmark, and she produced several champions who, in their turn, became the start for other kennels, such as Mr. F. Derwort's Pool of Buzzard and Mrs. M. Dingley's Laburnum. Mrs. H. v. d.

A working Springer of the 1990s in the Netherlands.

Brink's Van het Veense Springertje started with a Duin en Kruidberg bitch, which was mated to Norfolk's Moby Dick and is now well on its way. Snugglewood is the prefix of Mr. C. Warmenhoven, best known for their Cockers but they had a good run with their English Springers as well. Dutch Ch. Stowequest Trident Lad was an import who did very well in Holland, winning several Groups at international all-breed championship shows.

Nowadays the influence of Danish and Swedish breeding becomes more noted, two countries where the show Springers are of a very high standard.

In the field-trial lines, we see many more breeders of whom the most successful ones have been: Mr. G. Visscher's van het Eendebos, Mr. R. van Stuyvenberg's Dashhill, Mr. B. Boers' Hauk and Mr. J.

The top English Springer Spaniel in Holland in 1996, 1997 and 1998 was Dutch Ch. Stowequest Trident Lad, bred in England and owned by C. A. F. Warmenhoven in Holland.

23

The legendary Ch. Salilyn's Aristocrat was the top sire of all time, all breeds, as well as the winner of 45 Bests in Show and Top Dog of 1967.

Even as an older dog, Ch. Salilyn's Aristocrat was an elegant, prize-winning sire in the 1960s.

Wintermans v. d. Steevoerde. A famous import was Mr. van Stuyvenberg's Bonny of Gilcraig, who not only became a Dutch and international field trial champion herself but also was the dam of four field trial champions from two litters sired by Kentoo Donald.

One interesting phenomenon is the import of several "American-type" English Springers. In the early '90s, the first dogs arrived in Holland of whom Dutch Ch. Skywatch's Silverhill Elias became the best known. He was the second Springer to win a Best in Show at an all-breed show.

Although the American bloodlines are well represented in Germany (mainly through Scandinavian imports) and have been used by Scandinavian breeders, the American type has not become very popular in Holland where the English type of Springer still dominates.

In Holland and Germany, a dog that wins four CCs at championship shows becomes a champion. In Denmark, three CCs are sufficient. A dog becomes an international champion when he obtains a qualification in an international field trial as well. In France, he has to obtain a qualification in the field as well as three CCs at shows to become a champion. A field trial champion is a dog that has won two championships at an official field trial or one championship and two reserve championships and who, moreover, has obtained the

qualification "Very Good" or "Excellent" at a show.

THE ENGLISH SPRINGER IN AMERICA

It is interesting to note that the author of a book written in the early 1600s (*Journal of the English Plantation at Plymouth* by G. Mourt) reported that there were two dogs on board the Mayflower, a mastiff and a spaniel.

The Springer Spaniel has long been very popular in the United States. They were used to work in swamplands and brambles, just as in England. Later, because of the growing popularity of setters and pointers, their number declined to such an extent that the breed was

Ch. Salilyn's Condor was Top Dog All Breeds in 1992 and Best in Show at Westminster in 1993. Pictured is the Best in Show win.

threatened with extinction, but thanks to the Sporting Spaniel Society and the breeders it was saved. They set out to re-develop the Springer Spaniel by using the liver-and-white and black-and-white Keepers Spaniels, the Clumber, the old English Water Spaniel, the Sussex, the setter and spaniel-crosses that were owned by sportsmen. They succeeded and, as the breed revived, interest increased and many imports from the UK contributed to a wider genetic base for the breed.

The first official registration was in 1910 and the first show with classes for Springers was in 1923 in Madison Square Garden, New York, followed by the first field trial in 1924. Best of Breed at the show was Horsford Highness, a son of Horsford Hetman.

In 1924 the American Kennel Club recognized the standard for the English Springer Spaniel after the foundation of the English

Ch. Salilyn's Aristocrat's son, Ch. Adamant James, took Best in Show at the Westminster show, held in New York, in both 1971 and 1972.

25

English Springer Spaniel

Springer Spaniel Field Trial Association. In 1932 this standard was replaced by another.

Mr. Chevrier was a breed enthusiast who lived in Canada and it is for a great part thanks to him that the breed is so well established in the United States and Canada. In three-and-a-half years' time, up to 1925, he imported 250 dogs from England, including Field Trial Champion Flint of Avendale, Field Trial Champion Dan of Avendale, Ch. Springbok of Ware and many others. In 1925 there were 600 Springers in his kennels and at the Westminster Show he showed 11 Springers!

In the '50s and '60s a lot of good-quality English Springers found their way from Great Britain to the States, and since

then the breed has prospered. The most famous breeder in the United States was undoubtedly Mrs. Julia Gasow of the Salilyn prefix, and her most famous dog is Ch. Salilyn's Aristocrat, who won 45 Bests in Show, was number-one sire of all time, all breeds with 188 champion offspring. He was top dog in 1967. His grandson Ch. Salilyn's Private Stock and his great-grandson Ch. Salilyn's Classic each produced more than 100 champions. His son Ch. Chinoe's Adamant James won Best in Show at Westminster in 1971 and 1972. He was top dog in 1971. His great-grandson Ch. Salilyn's Condor was top dog all

Head studies of (left) an American dog and (right) a dog from the UK. The American Springer is the famous Ch. Salilyn's Aristocrat.

breeds in 1992 and Best in Show at Westminster in 1993.

As in England the gap between the show and working Springers has widened and could not be bridged anymore. Apart from that, the American breeders have nowadays created a show dog that has its own, very distinct type, and the difference between English and American Springer Spaniels has become just as notable as the difference between show and working type.

The American Springers are mostly all "open marked," i.e.,

black and white or liver and white without any ticking, they have more coat and are slightly more cocker-like in type, especially in head. They are slightly smaller (20 inches in the British standard and 18 inches in the American standard). Although different in type, it is without any doubt a beautiful dog and that is one of the reasons why fanciers of both the American and the English type suggested that the American Springer Spaniel be recognized as a separate breed.

27

Characteristics of the
ENGLISH SPRINGER SPANIEL

Once you have decided that you want to share your life with a dog, the next question is: which breed is it going to be? You must determine which breed suits you best in temperament and in lifestyle, and what do you plan to do with your new puppy? Do you want to work on your shape and physique with your dog? Would you like to do agility or obedience training or are you so fortunate as to be able to take a dog on a shoot?

English Springers are often the hunting dogs of choice because they are skilled workers with gentle mouths as well as pleasant companions. They are intelligent dogs and, thus, easily trained.

A Springer Spaniel is a happy, even-natured dog. Like all the other spaniels, he has the innate desire to please, which makes him a good dog to work with as well as a lovable companion. His is a faithful and cheerful personality. He is happy to work and happy to play; he is the ultimate optimist. He gets up every morning in the joyful expectation of another lovely day, with lots of fun, hopefully a lot to eat because he loves his food, and who knows what new and exciting adventures! If you take him on a walk, he will expect to find game behind every blade of grass, and in the show ring he will give his all for you. He loves to share his happiness with everybody, and if this means that he jumps up on you with four muddy paws, you have to understand that in the spirit with which it was done! His happy, easygoing temperament also makes him a fatalist. If he cannot come with you, he will express his great sorrow (and he can look very sorrowful!), but he will accept the situation and make the best of it. If his feet are to be trimmed, he will try to wriggle out of it; but if you are firm he will give a mental shrug and go to sleep on the grooming table. This behavior makes it very important that you are gentle but firm with him, because he is clever enough to realize that if he gets his way once, he may get it again and again.

Although your Springer may think that every guest to your house has been especially invited to please him and will therefore be loved by him, he is very loyal and affectionate to his own people. He not only shares your house he also shares your life, your joys and your sorrows. He has a special antenna for your moods. The bond between you and your Springer can become incredibly strong to the point that no words are needed.

ARE YOU A SPRINGER PERSON?
Other distinctions of the Springer that deserve mention is that he is the oldest of the sporting gundogs and that his original purpose was finding and springing game. Nowadays he is used for finding, flushing and retrieving game and he not only is very good at it but also loves to work for you.

This means that you have to provide an outlet for his active and lively nature. You must be prepared to give your Springer, when he has matured, at least an hour of free exercise every day. While he will enjoy a walk through the park on the lead, or even a shopping expedition, he needs to have the opportunity to stretch his legs, run at full speed and be able to pick up exciting smells that appeal to his hunting instinct. Woods, fields, dunes, he loves them all, but he especially loves water. If the idea of a soaking wet and muddy dog doesn't appeal to you, you have to teach him right from the start to stay away from the water. Don't think that will be easy! In the eyes of a Springer, a walk without a swim is only half a walk but, if necessary, a romp in a deep, preferably muddy puddle will also do!

Springers love the water! Walks and runs are great exercise, but the Springer will always welcome the opportunity to go for a swim.

29

English Springer Spaniel

Although a sporting dog by nature, the Springer makes a wonderful pet and is a popular choice for many families.

The Springer's energy is endless. He will walk the same distance as you do two or three times over, at full speed, without resting—and it only takes the ten-minute drive home in the car to restore him. Once home, he would like you to play with him, throw a ball for him to fetch or other activities to get rid of his energy.

In recent years the working ability of the breed has been extended and performances have improved in speed and style. This may bring the risk of exaggeration and you may end up with a hyperactive dog who is more diffi-cult to train. For the average owner, such a Springer is just a bit too much to cope with.

You have to make up your mind beforehand: will you want to train him for field trials? Then very likely a good Springer from sensible trainable lines will be the best all-round gundog for you

Do you want to show? Then find a breeder who breeds lovely and healthy Springers of good quality and you'll have a gentle companion who will love his outings with you and whose will to please makes him the perfect show dog.

Do you just want a pet? Then you can choose either but bear in mind that a Springer as a pet needs all the exercise and training a show or working Springer needs.

If you live in an apartment or in the center of a city, I would not recommend a Springer. They can adapt to any environment, but as working dogs they need open areas where they can have proper exercise and use their normal instincts for hunting and enjoying the scents of the countryside. Town parks and recreation fields are not enough.

Now that you have decided on a Springer Spaniel, there still are a few questions that need to be answered before you can go to a breeder. What color would you like? Will it be a dog or a bitch? It is often said that a bitch is sweeter than a dog, but in my experience the dogs are just as sweet as the bitches and very easygoing. It is very important that you explain all your preferences to the breeder so that he can help you pick the puppy that is best suited to you.

If you have a family with children, it might be wiser not to buy a dominant puppy because the puppy will have several "masters" and will end up not listening to anybody. In a slightly dominant dog, that may cause problems! In a litter the personalities of the puppies may differ slightly. Explain to the breeder what you prefer: the softer, sweeter one, or the outgoing, feisty puppy?

If you have the time and dedication to train your puppy and treat him consistently at all times, there is no better pet than an English Springer Spaniel. By choosing an English Springer Spaniel, you have chosen a companion with a very happy temperament, who thinks life is wonderful and who will love you indiscriminately.

COAT COLORS

Dr. Caius mentioned in his *Treatise of Dogges* (1570), the *Aquaticus* or *Spanyell* who finds game in the water and who is either red and white, solid black or solid red. In 1803 in the book *The Sportsman's Cabinet*, springing spaniels and cocking spaniels are mentioned in the colors black and white, liver and white and red and white.

In 1933 the English Springer Spaniel Club decided that all the colors of the original land spaniels would be permissible

with the exception of the typical red and white which is restricted to the Welsh Springer Spaniels. Thus the official colors for the English Springer Spaniels are black and white, liver and white, black, white and tan and liver, white and tan.

Although either black and white or liver and white (with or without tan markings) is allowed, the popular color has always been, and still is, liver and white with or without ticking.

Regardless of the color of the Springer puppy, this is an adorable beautiful breed of sporting dog.

31

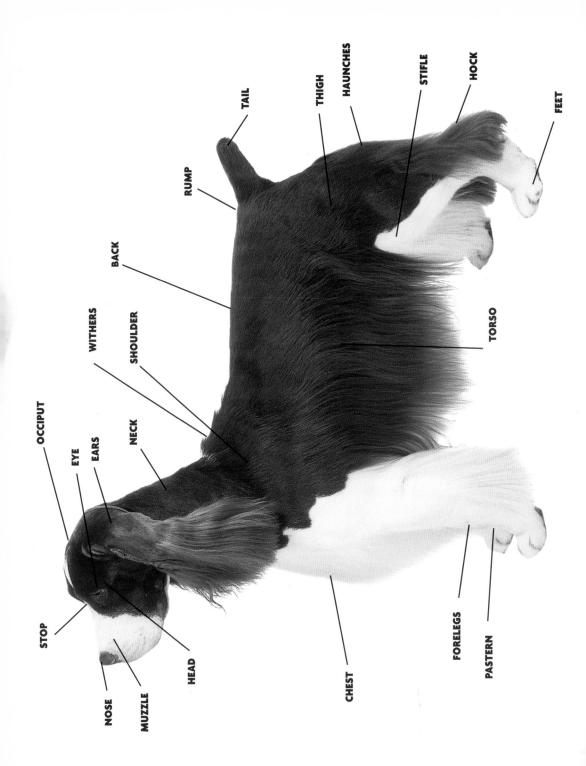

OCCIPUT

STOP

EYE

EARS

NECK

WITHERS

SHOULDER

BACK

RUMP

TAIL

THIGH

HAUNCHES

STIFLE

HOCK

FEET

TORSO

NOSE

MUZZLE

HEAD

STOP

CHEST

FORELEGS

PASTERN

ENGLISH SPRINGER SPANIEL

Following we present an excerpt from the American Kennel Club (AKC) breed standard, which effectively describes the desirable conformation of the Springer. A standard is used by breeders and show judges alike as a "blueprint" of the ideal representative of the breed.

THE AMERICAN KENNEL CLUB STANDARD FOR THE ENGLISH SPRINGER SPANIEL

General Appearance: The English Springer Spaniel is a medium-sized sporting dog, with a compact body and a docked tail. His coat is moderately long, with feathering on his legs, ears, chest and brisket. His pendulous ears, soft gentle expression, sturdy build and friendly wagging tail proclaim him unmistakably a member of the ancient family of Spaniels. He is above all a well-proportioned dog, free from exaggeration, nicely balanced in every part. His carriage is proud and upstanding, body deep, legs strong and muscular, with enough length to carry him with ease. Taken as a whole, the English Springer Spaniel suggests power, endurance and agility. He looks the part of a dog that can go, and keep going, under difficult hunting conditions. At his best, he is endowed with style, symmetry, balance and enthusiasm, and is every inch a sporting dog of distinct spaniel character, combining beauty and utility.

Size, Proportion, Substance: The Springer is built to cover rough ground with agility and reasonable speed. His structure suggests the capacity for endurance. He is

Well proportioned, compact and medium sized, the English Springer should convey style, symmetry and balance.

33

Head study, showing pleasing type, structure and proportion.

and refinement. It is important that its size and proportion be in balance with the rest of the dog. Viewed in profile, the head appears approximately the same length as the neck and blends with the body in substance. The stop, eyebrows and chiseling of the bony structure around the eye sockets contribute to the Springer's beautiful and characteristic expression, which is alert, kindly and trusting. The eyes, more than any other feature, are the essence of the Springer's appeal. Correct size, shape,

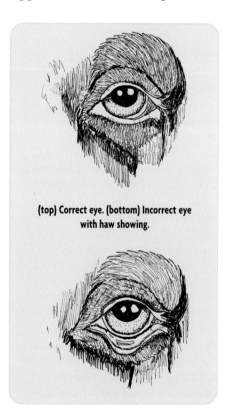

(top) Correct eye. (bottom) Incorrect eye with haw showing.

to be kept to medium size. Ideal height at the shoulder for dogs is 20 inches; for bitches, it is 19 inches. A 20-inch dog, well-proportioned and in good condition, will weigh approximately 50 pounds; a 19-inch bitch will weigh approximately 40 pounds. The length of the body (measured from point of shoulder to point of buttocks) is slightly greater than the height at the withers. A Springer with correct substance appears well-knit and sturdy with good bone, however, he is never coarse or ponderous.

Head: The head is impressive without being heavy. Its beauty lies in a combination of strength

placement and color influence expression and attractiveness. The eyes are of medium size and oval in shape, set rather well-apart and fairly deep in their sockets. The color of the iris harmonizes with the color of the coat, preferably dark hazel in the liver and white dogs and black or deep brown in the black and white dogs. Eyerims are fully pigmented and match the coat in color. Lids are tight with little or no haw showing. Ears are long and fairly wide, hanging close to the cheeks with no tendency to stand up or out. The ear leather is thin and approximately long enough to reach the tip of the nose. Correct ear set is on a level with the eye and not too far back on the skull. The skull is medium-length and fairly broad, flat on top and slightly rounded at the sides and back. The occiput bone is inconspicuous. The amount of stop is moderate. The muzzle is approximately the same length as the skull and one-half the width of the skull. The nasal bone is straight, with no inclination downward toward the tip of the nose, the latter giving an undesirable downfaced look. The cheeks are flat, and the face is well-chiseled under the eyes. Jaws are of sufficient length to allow the dog to carry game easily: fairly square, lean and strong. The nose is fully pigmented, liver or black in color, depending on the color

Body profile, showing correct structure, balance and type with a mature coat properly groomed.

of the coat. The nostrils are well-opened and broad. Teeth are strong, clean, of good size and ideally meet in a close scissors bite. An even bite or one or two incisors slightly out of line are minor faults.

Neck, Topline, Body: The neck is moderately long, muscular, clean and slightly arched at the crest. It blends gradually and smoothly into sloping shoulders. The portion of the topline from withers to tail is firm and slopes very gently. The body is short-coupled, strong and compact. The chest is deep, reaching the level of the elbows, with well-developed forechest; however, it is not so wide or round as to interfere with the action of the front legs. The back is straight, strong and essentially level. Loins are strong, short and slightly arched. Hips are nicely rounded, blending smoothly into the hind legs. The croup slopes gently to the set of the tail, and tail-set follows the natural line of the croup. The tail is carried horizontally or slightly elevated and displays a characteristic lively, merry action, particularly when the dog is on game.

FAULTS IN PROFILE

Left: Snipey muzzle, generally lacking substance and bone, narrow front, upright shoulders, soft topline, high in rear, lacking angulation behind, low tail set and carriage.
Right: Short, heavy muzzle, bumpy topskull, short thick neck, low on leg, excessive coat exaggerating coarseness, overangulated in rear, upright, loaded shoulders.

Left: Ears set on too high, short neck, excessive dewlap, heavy, upright shoulders, weak topline, steep in croup, low tail set, lacking angulation in rear, low on leg, flat feet.
Right: Thin, apple-headed, ewe-necked, long back, gay tail, weak pasterns, toes out in front, lacking bone, overly sloping topline.

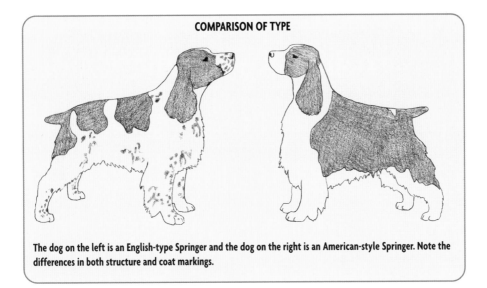

COMPARISON OF TYPE

The dog on the left is an English-type Springer and the dog on the right is an American-style Springer. Note the differences in both structure and coat markings.

Forequarters: The shoulder blades are flat and fairly close together at the tips, molding smoothly into the contour of the body. Elbows lie close to the body. Forelegs are straight with the same degree of size continuing to the foot. Pasterns are short, strong and slightly sloping, with no suggestion of weakness. Dewclaws are usually removed. Feet are round or slightly oval. They are compact and well-arched, of medium size with thick pads, and well-feathered between the toes.

Hindquarters: His whole rear assembly suggests strength and driving power. Thighs are broad and muscular. Stifle joints are strong. For functional efficiency, the angulation of the hindquarter is never greater than that of the

forequarter, and not appreciably less. The hock joints are somewhat rounded, not small and sharp in contour. Rear pasterns are short and strong, with good bone. When viewed from behind, the rear pasterns are parallel. Dewclaws are usually removed. The feet are the same as in front, except that they are smaller and often more compact.

Coat: On the body, the outer coat is of medium length, flat or wavy, and is easily distinguishable from the undercoat, which is short, soft and dense. The quantity of undercoat is affected by climate and season. When in combination, outer coat and undercoat serve to make the dog substantially waterproof, weatherproof and thornproof. On ears, chest, legs and

The coat of the English Springer Spaniel should appear clean and glossy; it is of medium length, either flat or wavy.

equally acceptable:(1) Black or liver with white markings or predominantly white with black or liver markings; (2) Blue or liver roan; (3) Tricolor: black and white or liver and white with tan markings, usually found on eyebrows, cheeks, inside of ears and under the tail. Any white portion of the coat may be flecked with ticking. Off colors such as lemon, red or orange are not to place.

belly, the Springer is nicely furnished with a fringe of feathering of moderate length and heaviness. On the head, front of the forelegs, and below the hock joints on the front of the hind legs, the hair is short and fine. The coat has the clean, glossy, "live" appearance indicative of good health. It is legitimate to trim about the head, ears, neck and feet, to remove dead undercoat, and to thin and shorten excess feathering as required to enhance a smart, functional appearance. The tail may be trimmed, or well fringed with wavy feathering. Above all, the appearance should be natural. Correct quality and condition of coat is to take precedence over quantity of coat.

Color: All the following combinations of colors and markings are

Gait: The front and rear assemblies must be equivalent in angulation and muscular development for the gait to be smooth and effortless. Shoulders which are well laid-back to permit a long stride are just as essential as the excellent rear quarters that provide driving power. Seen from the side, the Springer exhibits a long, ground-covering stride and carries a firm back, with no tendency to dip, roach or roll from side to side. Movement faults include high-stepping, wasted motion; short, choppy stride; crabbing; and moving with the feet wide, the latter giving roll or swing to the body.

Temperament: The typical Springer is friendly, eager to please, quick to learn and willing to obey. Such traits are conducive to tractability, which is essential for appropriate handler control in the field.

The English Springer Spaniel is friendly and willing to please, especially with well-behaved young people.

39

ENGLISH SPRINGER SPANIEL

FINDING A BREEDER

Once you have decided that it is an English Springer with whom you want to share your life, your next step is to find a breeder. It may help you to visit a couple of dog shows or breed club matches. Watch the breeders and how they communicate with their dogs, look at the dogs and see which breeder has dogs with the type and temperament that you like. You can also contact the breed club and ask for names and addresses of breeders with puppies for sale. The club will give you a list of breeders who have puppies that fulfill the club rules. These rules mainly concern matters of hereditary defects in both parents.

TEMPERAMENT COUNTS

Your selection of a good puppy can be determined by your needs. A show potential or a good pet? It is your choice. Every puppy, however, should be of good temperament. Although show-quality puppies are bred and raised with emphasis on physical conformation, responsible breeders strive for equally good temperament. Do not buy from a breeder who concentrates solely on physical beauty at the expense of personality.

If the breeders whose dogs you like are not on the list, do not hesitate to contact them and ask if they will have puppies in the future and whether these puppies will fulfill the club rules. If you visit a breeder and you are a bit doubtful about the puppies or the breeder or the conditions in which the puppies are kept, or if the breeder thinks that checking for hereditary defects is not necessary, don't buy! It must be a 100% decision. Buying a pup because you are afraid to say no or because you feel sorry for the pup is wrong. After all, you are going to buy a companion who will live for the next 12–14 years and you must be absolutely sure that he is the one you want and no other!

Although the English Springer Spaniel is a healthy breed, there are a few breed-related hereditary conditions. Responsible breeders will have their stock examined for these conditions and will not breed from affected stock. Defects that can sometimes occur are:

Hip dysplasia is a degeneration of the hip socket into which the femoral head rests. It is common in most breeds of pure-bred dogs.

Progressive retinal atrophy is a congenital disease of the eye that affects the Springer as well as many other pure-bred dogs.

Cataracts, a condition whereby the lens will become covered with a milky film, is often seen in older dogs (ten years and older). Since aging is a gradual process, it is not much cause for urgent concern when a cataract begins to form. However, there is another form of cataract that occurs at an early age, affecting the eyesight of the dog and therefore is much more serious.

Retinal dysplasia, another eye condition, in its mildest form is seen as a multiple folding of the retina that has no influence on the eyesight, and in its most serious form is a non-attachment of the retina to the underlying choroid and can lead to blindness.

Should you want to buy a puppy for showing, discuss with the breeder what to do in case the puppy will not be showable. Its mouth may go wrong, if it's a male he may turn out to be monorchid (only one descended testicle), etc. If you are very determined to have a show-quality pup, you might do better to buy a more mature puppy, say six to seven months, so that these risks cannot occur. Inquire about inoculations and when the puppy was last dosed for worms.

Nowadays puppies are often sold with a sales contract. This is fine, but don't sign on the spot. Ask the breeder if you can take it

Children and puppies naturally make the best of friends! When choosing a puppy, all members of the family should participate in the decision.

home to read it carefully so that you know exactly what you are signing. More important than a sales contract, however, is a good relationship between

TIME TO GO HOME

Breeders rarely release puppies until they are eight to ten weeks of age. This is an acceptable age for most breeds of dog, excepting toy breeds, which are not released until around 12 weeks, given their petite sizes. If a breeder has a puppy that is 12 weeks of age or older, it is likely well socialized and house-trained. Be sure that it is otherwise healthy before deciding to take it home.

41

you and the breeder. A responsible, dedicated breeder is at all times willing to answer all your questions, to calm your fears and to share your joys.

SELECTING A PUPPY

You contacted a breeder, he has a litter and there you are, surrounded by all these adorable puppies. How will you ever be able to choose! You have decided that you want a bitch puppy so ask the breeder to take the dog puppies away, that makes it a bit easier. Now what you are looking for is a healthy, good-looking, happy little thing that will be all over you when you crouch down, thinking you are great fun. Don't go for shy puppies but don't go for the bullies either! Ask the breeder if you can see the dam (and sire, if possible) and see what her temperament is like.

PUPPY APPEARANCE
Your puppy should have a well-fed appearance but not a distended abdomen, which may indicate worms or incorrect feeding, or both. The body should be firm, with a solid feel. The skin of the abdomen should be pale pink and clean, without signs of scratching or rash. Check the hind legs to make certain that dewclaws were removed.

Discuss the pedigree with him, so that you can make sure that your puppy comes from good stock accomplished in the show ring or field.

A ten-week-old Springer puppy should have a fairly long head with a well-defined stop, a good reach of neck, good ribs and good quarters with hocks well let down. Shoulders should be laid back, front legs straight. The set of the tail should be a little below the level of the back and should be carried straight with lively action.

The puppy should have nice tight dark eyes. Take care to look for damp patches around the eyes because that means that there is something amiss. A good shiny coat is an indication of good health as is a happy and exuberant temperament.

Remember, you cannot be too careful when it comes to deciding on the type of dog you want and finding out about your prospective pup's background. Buying a puppy is not—or should not be—just another whimsical purchase. In fact, this is one instance in which you actually do get to choose your own family! But, you may be thinking, buying a puppy should be fun—it should not be so serious and so much work. Keep in mind that your puppy is not a cuddly stuffed toy or decorative lawn ornament, but instead will

The decision can be difficult when choosing an adorable Springer puppy.

become a real member of your family. Thus, you will realize that, while buying a puppy is a pleasurable and exciting endeavor, it is not something to be taken lightly. Relax...the fun will start when the pup comes home!

Bear in mind that a puppy is nothing more than a baby in a furry disguise...a baby who is virtually helpless in a human world and who trusts his owner for fulfillment of his basic needs for survival. That goes beyond

YOUR SCHEDULE . . .
If you lead an erratic, unpredictable life, with daily or weekly changes in your work requirements, consider the problems of owning a puppy. The new puppy has to be fed regularly, socialized (loved, petted, handled, introduced to other people) and, most importantly, allowed to go outdoors for house-training. As the dog gets older, he can be more tolerant of deviations in his feeding and relief schedule.

43

Within a few day's time, your Springer puppy will begin to feel at home in his new surroundings.

never hurts to emphasize the commitment of dog ownership. With some time and patience, it is really not too difficult to raise a curious and exuberant Springer Spaniel pup to be a well-adjusted and well-mannered adult dog—a dog that could be your most loyal friend.

PREPARING PUPPY'S PLACE IN YOUR HOME

Researching your breed and finding a breeder are only two aspects of the "homework" you will have to do before bringing your puppy home. You will also have to prepare your home and family for the new addition. Much like you would prepare a nursery for a newborn baby, you will need to designate a place in your home that will be the puppy's own. How you prepare your home will depend on how much freedom the dog will be allowed. Whatever you decide, you must ensure that

food, water and shelter; your pup needs care, protection, guidance and love. If you are not prepared to commit to this, then you are not prepared to own a dog.

Do not worry too much as you will probably find that once your pup gets used to his new home, he will fall into his place in the family quite naturally. But it

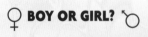

♀ BOY OR GIRL? ♂

An important consideration to be discussed is the sex of your puppy. For a family companion, a bitch may be the better choice, considering the female's inbred concern for all young creatures and her accompanying tolerance and patience. It is always advised to spay a pet bitch, which may guarantee her a longer life.

he has a place that he can "call his own."

When you bring your new puppy into your home, you are bringing him into what will become his home as well. Obviously, you did not buy a puppy so that he could take control of your house, but in order for a puppy to grow into a stable, well-adjusted dog, he has to feel comfortable in his surroundings. Remember, he is leaving the warmth and security of his dam and littermates, as well as the familiarity of the only place he has ever known, so it is important to make his transition as easy as possible. By preparing a place in your home

PEDIGREE VS. REGISTRATION CERTIFICATE

Too often new owners are confused between these two important documents. Your puppy's pedigree, essentially a family tree, is a written record of a dog's genealogy of three generations or more. The pedigree will show you the names as well as performance titles of all the dogs in your pup's background. Your breeder must provide you with a registration application, with his part properly filled out. You must complete the application and send it to the AKC with the proper fee. Every puppy must come from a litter that has been AKC-registered by the breeder, born in the USA and from sire and dam that are also registered with the AKC.

The seller must provide you with complete records to identify the puppy. The AKC requires that the seller provide the buyer with the following: breed; sex, color and markings; date of birth; litter number (when available); names and registration numbers of the parents; breeder's name; and date sold or delivered.

You should be prepared with a suitable crate, toys, water and food bowls and a few other essentials *before* you bring home the English Springer Spaniel.

for the puppy, you are making him feel as welcome as possible in a strange new place. It should not take him long to get used to it, but the sudden shock of being transplanted is somewhat traumatic for a young pup. Imagine how a small child would feel in the same situation—that is how your puppy must be feeling. It is up to you to reassure him and to let him know, "Little fellow, you are going to like it here!"

WHAT YOU SHOULD BUY
CRATE

To someone unfamiliar with the use of crates in dog training, it may seem like punishment to shut a dog in a crate, but this is not the case at all. Most breeders recommend a crate as a preferred

PHOTO COURTESY OF DOSKOCIL.

tool for pet puppies as well as show puppies. Crates are not cruel—crates have many humane and highly effective uses in dog care and training. For example, crate training is a very popular and very successful housebreaking method. A crate can keep your dog safe during travel; and, perhaps most importantly, a crate provides your dog with a place of his own in your home. It serves as a "doggie bedroom" of sorts—your Springer can curl up in his crate when he wants to sleep or when he just needs a break.

> ### ARE YOU PREPARED?
> Unfortunately, when a puppy is bought by someone who does not take into consideration the time and attention that dog ownership requires, it is the puppy who suffers when he is either abandoned or placed in a shelter by a frustrated owner. So all of the "home-work" you do in preparation for your pup's arrival will benefit you both. The more informed you are, the more you will know what to expect and the better equipped you will be to handle the ups and downs of raising a puppy. Hopefully, everyone in the household is willing to do his part in raising and caring for the pup. The anticipation of owning a dog often brings a lot of promises from excited family members: "I will walk him every day," "I will feed him," "I will house-train him," etc., but these things take time and effort, and promises can easily be forgotten once the novelty of the new pet has worn off.

Many dogs sleep in their crates overnight. When equipped with soft bedding and his favorite toy, a crate becomes a cozy pseudo-den for your dog. Like his ancestors, he too will seek out the comfort and retreat of a den—you just happen to be providing him with something a little more luxurious than his early ancestors enjoyed.

As far as purchasing a crate, the type that you buy is up to you. It will likely be one of the two most popular types: wire or fiberglass. There are advantages and disadvantages to each type.

For example, a wire crate is more open, allowing the air to flow through and affording the dog a view of what is going on around him while a fiberglass crate is sturdier. Both can double as travel crates, providing protection for the dog. The size of the crate is another thing to consider. Puppies do not stay puppies forever—in fact, sometimes it seems as if they grow right before your eyes. A small-sized crate may be fine for a very young Springer pup, but it will not do him much good for long! Unless you have the money and

Breeders often raise pups on newspaper to initiate the house-training process. Avoid using newspaper at home unless you intend to have the pup eliminate indoors.

Puppies need to chew, and they will chew anything! They require safe chew toys to divert their attention from your belongings and items that could be dangerous.

the inclination to buy a new crate every time your pup has a growth spurt, it is better to get one that will accommodate your dog both as a pup and at full size. A medium-size crate will be necessary for a full-grown English Springer Spaniel, who stands approximately 20 inches high.

Tug toys are ideal for puppies because you can initiate a game with your pup as part of the bonding experience. While gentle play with tug toys is good, you should never incite your pup into an aggressive tug-of-war game.

GROWING PAINS

The majority of problems that are commonly seen in young pups will disappear as your dog gets older. However, how you deal with problems when he is young will determine how he reacts to discipline as an adult dog. It is important to establish who is boss (hopefully it will be you!) right away when you are first bonding with your dog. This bond will set the tone for the rest of your life together.

BEDDING

A nice lambs' wool pad in the dog's crate will help the dog feel more at home and you may also like to offer the pup a small blanket. This will take the place of the leaves, twigs, etc., that the pup would use in the wild to make a den; the pup can make his own "burrow" in the crate. Although your pup is far removed from his den-making ancestors, the denning instinct is still a part of his genetic makeup. Second, until you bring your pup home, he has been sleeping amid the warmth of his dam and littermates, and while a blanket is not the same as a warm, breathing body, it still provides heat and something with which to snuggle. You will want to wash your pup's bedding

frequently in case he has an accident in his crate, and replace or remove any bedding that becomes ragged and starts to fall apart.

Toys

Toys are a must for dogs of all ages, especially for curious playful pups. Puppies are the "children" of the dog world, and what child does not love toys? Chew toys provide enjoyment to both dog and owner—your dog will enjoy playing with his favorite toys, while you will enjoy the fact that they distract him from your expensive shoes and leather sofa. Puppies love to chew; in fact, chewing is a physical need for pups as they are teething, and everything looks appetizing! The full range of your possessions— from old dishcloth to Oriental rug—are fair game in the eyes of a teething pup. Puppies are not all that discerning when it comes to

Your local pet shop will have a wide variety of leads in many colors, materials and thicknesses. Select a durable lead that will last you and your Springer many years.

finding something to literally "sink their teeth into"—everything tastes great!

Breeders advise owners to resist stuffed toys, because they

PHOTO COURTESY OF MIKKI PET PRODUCTS.

PET INSURANCE

Just like you can insure your car, your house and your own health, you likewise can insure your dog's health. Investigate a pet insurance policy by talking to your vet. Depending on the age of your dog, the breed and the kind of coverage you desire, your policy can be very affordable. Most policies cover accidental injuries, poisoning, and thousands of medical problems and illnesses, including cancers. Some carriers also offer routine care and immunization coverage.

There are many high-quality toys made especially for dogs. Only buy toys made for canines, as toys made for human children are not strong enough to withstand puppy teeth.

49

can become de-stuffed in no time. The overly excited pup may ingest the stuffing, which is neither digestible nor nutritious. Similarly, squeaky toys are quite popular, but if a pup "disembowels" one of these, the small plastic squeaker inside can be dangerous if swallowed.

Be careful of natural bones, which have a tendency to splinter into sharp, dangerous pieces. Also be careful of rawhide, which can turn into pieces that are easy to swallow or into a mushy mess on your carpet. Most puppies love the calf hooves that you can buy in any pet shop or at shows. They can chew for hours on them without coming to any harm. However, if what's left of the hoof becomes too small, you'd better

THE RIDE HOME
Taking your dog from the breeder to your home in a car can be a very uncomfortable experience for both of you. The puppy will have been taken from his warm, friendly, safe environment and brought into a strange new environment—an environment that moves! Be prepared for loose bowels, urination, crying, whining and even fear biting. With proper love and encouragement when you arrive home, the stress of the trip should quickly disappear.

take it away. Monitor the condition of all your pup's toys carefully and get rid of any that have been chewed to the point of becoming potentially dangerous.

LEAD
A nylon lead is probably the best option as it is the most resistant to puppy teeth. Many a Springer puppy will take a liking to chewing on his lead. Of course, this is a habit that should be "nipped" in the bud. Nylon leads are strong but lightweight, which is good for a young Springer puppy who is just getting used to the idea of walking on a lead. For everyday walking and safety purposes, the nylon lead is a good choice. As your pup grows up and gets used to walking on the lead, you may want to purchase a flexible lead. These leads allow you to extend the length to give the dog a broader area to explore or to shorten the length to keep the dog close to you.

COLLAR
Your pup should get used to wearing a collar all the time since you will want to attach his ID tags to it. A lightweight nylon collar is a good choice. Make sure that it fits snugly enough so that the pup cannot wriggle out of it, but is loose enough so that it will not be uncomfortably tight around the pup's neck. You

Choose the Right Collar

The **BUCKLE COLLAR** is the standard collar used for everyday purposes. Be sure that you adjust the buckle on growing puppies. Check it every day. It can become too tight overnight! These collars can be made of leather or nylon. Attach your dog's identification tags to this collar.

The **CHOKE CHAIN** is designed for training. It is constructed of highly polished steel so that it slides easily through the stainless steel loop. The idea is that the dog controls the pressure around his neck and he will stop pulling if the collar becomes uncomfortable. Never leave a choke collar on your dog when not training.

The **HALTER** is for a trained dog that has to be restrained to prevent running away, chasing a cat and the like. Considered the most humane of all collars, it is frequently used on smaller dogs on which collars are not comfortable.

Provide your English Springer Spaniel with food and water bowls. These bowls can be constructed of sturdy plastic, ceramic, clay or stainless steel.

PHOTO COURTESY OF MIKKI PET PRODUCTS.

ELECTRICAL FENCING

The electrical fencing system which forms an invisible fence works on a battery-operated collar that shocks the dog if it gets too close to the buried (or elevated) wire. There are some people who think very highly of this system of controlling a dog's wandering. Keep in mind that the collar has batteries. For safety's sake, replace the batteries every month with the best quality batteries available.

should be able to fit a finger between the pup and the collar. It may take some time for your pup to get used to wearing the collar, but soon he will not even notice that it is there. Choke collars are made for training, but should only be used by an experienced handler.

FOOD AND WATER BOWLS

Your pup will need two bowls, one for food and one for water. You may want two sets of bowls, one for inside and one for outside, depending on where the dog will be fed and where he will be spending most of his time. Stainless steel bowls that can be sterilized are good, but the sturdy special spaniel bowls whose shape allows the ears to fall outside the bowl are popular choices. These bowls avoid messy

chewed by puppy teeth and you do not want your dog to be constantly chewing apart his bowl (for his safety and for your wallet!).

CLEANING SUPPLIES

Until a pup is house-trained, you will be doing a lot of cleaning. Accidents will occur, which is okay in the beginning because the puppy does not know any better. All you can do is be prepared to clean up any accidents. Old rags, paper towels, newspapers and a safe disinfectant are good to have on hand.

Responsible, law-abiding dog owners pick up their dogs' droppings whenever they are in public. Pooper-scooper devices make the job quick and easy.

ears after the dinner and a wet floor after drinking! Plastic bowls are very chewable and therefore not advisable. Some dog owners like to put their dogs' food and water bowls on a specially made elevated stand. This brings the food closer to the dog's level so he does not have to bend down as far, thus aiding his digestion and helping to guard against bloat or gastric torsion in deep-chested dogs. The most important thing is to buy sturdy bowls since, again, anything is in danger of being

CRATE-TRAINING TIPS

During crate training, you should partition off the section of the crate in which the pup stays. If he is given too big an area, this will hinder your training efforts. Crate training is based on the fact that a dog does not like to soil his sleeping quarters, so it is ineffective to keep a pup in a crate that is so big that he can eliminate in one end and get far enough away from it to sleep. Also, you want to make the crate den-like for the pup. Blankets and a favorite toy will make the crate cozy for the small pup; as he grows, you may want to evict some of his "roommates" to make more room. It will take some coaxing at first, but be patient. Given some time to get used to it, your pup will adapt to his new home-within-a-home quite nicely.

BEYOND THE BASICS

The items previously discussed are the bare necessities. You will find out what else you need as you go along—grooming supplies, flea/tick protection, baby gates to partition a room, etc. These things will vary depending on your situation but it is important that you have everything you need to feed and make your Springer comfortable in his first few days at home.

PUPPY-PROOFING YOUR HOME

Aside from making sure that your English Springer Spaniel will be comfortable in your home, you also have to make sure that your home is safe for your Springer. This means taking precautions

NATURAL TOXINS

Examine your grass and landscaping before bringing your puppy home. Many varieties of plants have leaves, stems or flowers that are toxic if ingested, and you can depend on a curious puppy to investigate them. Ask your vet for information on poisonous plants or research them at your library.

that your pup will not get into anything he should not and that there is nothing within his reach that may harm him should he sniff it, chew it, inspect it, etc. This probably seems obvious since, while you are primarily concerned with your pup's safety, at the same time you do not want your belongings to be ruined. Breakables should be placed out of reach if your dog is to have full run of the house. If he is to be limited to certain places within the house, keep any potentially dangerous items in the "off-limits" areas. An electrical cord can pose a danger should the puppy decide to taste it—and who is going to convince a pup that it would not make a great chew toy? Cords should be fastened tightly against the wall. If your dog is going to spend time in a crate, make sure that there is nothing near his crate that he can reach if he sticks his curious little nose or paws through the openings. Just

An average home contains many potential dangers for a curious pup...a fireplace is just one example. The house should be puppy-proofed *before* bringing the pup home, and constant supervision is necessary.

as you would with a child, keep all household cleaners and chemicals where the pup cannot get to them.

It is also important to make sure that the outside of your home is safe. Of course your puppy should never be unsupervised, but a pup let loose in the yard will want to run and explore, and he should be granted that freedom. Do not let a fence give you a false sense of security; you would be surprised how crafty (and persistent) a dog can be in figuring out how to dig under and squeeze his way through small holes, or to jump or climb over a fence. The remedy is to make the fence high enough so that it really is impossible for your dog to get over it (about 6 feet should suffice), and well embedded into the ground. Be sure to repair or secure any gaps in the fence. Check the fence periodically to ensure that it is in good shape and make repairs as needed; a very determined pup may return to the same spot to "work on it" until he is able to get through.

FIRST TRIP TO THE VET

You have picked out your puppy, and your home and family are ready. Something else you need to prepare is your pup's first trip to the veterinarian. Perhaps the breeder can recommend someone in the area who specializes in Springer Spaniels, or maybe you

know some other dog owners who can suggest a good vet. Either way, you should have an appointment arranged for your pup before you pick him up and plan on taking him for an exami-

An active Springer pup will love to spend time running and playing in the yard, so make sure that the yard is safe for the puppy.

TOXIC PLANTS
Many plants can be toxic to dogs. If you see your dog carrying a piece of vegetation in his mouth, approach him in a quiet, disinterested manner, avoid eye contact, pet him and gradually remove the plant from his mouth. Alternatively, offer him a treat and maybe he'll drop the plant on his own accord. Be sure no toxic plants are growing in your own garden.

nation before bringing him home.

The pup's first visit will consist of an overall examination to make sure that the pup does not have any problems that are not apparent to you. The veterinarian will also set up a schedule for the pup's vaccinations; the breeder will inform you of which ones the pup has already received and the vet can continue from there.

INTRODUCTION TO THE FAMILY

Everyone in the house will be excited about the puppy's coming home and will want to pet him and play with him, but it is best to make the introductions low-key so as not to overwhelm the puppy. He is apprehensive already. It is the first time he has been separated from his dam and the breeder, and the ride to your home is likely the first time he has been in a car. The last thing you want to do is

smother him, as this will only frighten him further. This is not to say that human contact is not extremely necessary at this stage, because this is the time when a connection between the pup and his human family is formed. Gentle petting and soothing words should help console him, as well as just putting him down and letting him explore on his own (under your watchful eye, of course).

The pup may approach the family members or may busy himself with exploring for a while. Gradually, each person should spend some time with the pup, one at a time, crouching down to get as close to the pup's level as possible and letting him sniff their hands and petting him gently. He definitely needs human attention and he needs to be touched—this is how to form an immediate bond. Just remember that the pup is experiencing a lot of things for the first time, at the same time. There are new people, new noises, new smells and new things to investigate: so be gentle, be affectionate and be as comforting as you can.

YOUR PUP'S FIRST NIGHT HOME

You have traveled home with your new charge safely in his crate or on a new friend's lap. He's been to the vet for a thorough checkup; he's been

CHEMICAL TOXINS

Scour your garage for potential puppy dangers. Remove weed killers, pesticides and antifreeze materials. Antifreeze is highly toxic and just a few drops can kill a puppy or an adult dog. The sweet taste attracts the animal, who will quickly consume it from the floor or pavement.

PUPPY-PROOFING

Thoroughly puppy-proof your house before bringing your puppy home. Never use roach or rodent poisons in any area accessible to the puppy. Avoid the use of toilet bowl cleaners. Most dogs are born with toilet bowl sonar and will take a drink if the lid is left open. Also keep the trash secured and out of reach.

weighed, his papers examined; perhaps he's even been vaccinated and wormed as well. He's met the family, licked the whole family, including the excited children and the less-than-happy cat. He's explored his area, his new bed, the yard and anywhere else he's been permitted. He's eaten his first meal at home and relieved himself in the proper

Even very young children should be taught to treat pets with care and respect. A child who grows up around dogs will naturally accept them as part of the family.

57

These Springer pups have a great opportunity for socialization with their dam, littermates, other dogs and people of different ages.

place. He's heard lots of new sounds, smelled new friends and seen more of the outside world than ever before.

That was just the first day! He's worn out and is ready for bed...or so you think!

It's puppy's first night and you are ready to say "Good night"—keep in mind that this is puppy's first night ever to be sleeping alone. His dam and littermates are no longer at paw's length and he's a bit scared, cold and lonely. Be reassuring to your new family member. This is not the time to spoil him and give in to his inevitable whining.

Puppies whine. They whine to let the others know where they are and hopefully to get company out of it. Place your pup in his new bed or crate in his room and close the door. Mercifully, he may

FEEDING TIPS

You will probably start feeding your pup the same food that he has been getting from the breeder; the breeder should give you a few days' supply to start you off. Although you should not give your pup too many treats, you will want to have puppy treats on hand for coaxing, training, rewards, etc. Be careful, though, as a small pup's calorie requirements are relatively low and a few treats can add up to almost a full day's worth of calories without the required nutrition.

fall asleep without a peep. When the inevitable occurs, ignore the whining: he is fine. Be strong and keep his interest in mind. Do not allow your heart to become guilty and visit the pup. He will fall asleep.

Many breeders recommend placing a piece of bedding from his former homestead in his new bed so that he recognizes the scent of his littermates. Others still advise placing a hot water bottle in his bed for warmth. This latter may be a good idea provided the pup doesn't attempt to suckle—he'll get good and wet and may not fall asleep so fast.

Puppy's first night can be somewhat stressful for the pup and his new family. Remember that you are setting the tone of nighttime at your house. Unless you want to play with your pup every night at 10 p.m., midnight and 2 a.m., don't initiate the habit. Your family will thank you, and so will your pup!

PREVENTING PUPPY PROBLEMS
SOCIALIZATION
Now that you have done all of the preparatory work and have helped your pup get accustomed to his new home and family, it is about time for you to have some fun! Socializing your English Springer Spaniel pup gives you the opportunity to show off your new friend, and your pup gets to reap the benefits of being an adorable furry creature that people will want to pet and, in general, think is absolutely precious!

Besides getting to know his new family, your puppy should be exposed to other people, animals and situations, but of course he must not come into close contact with dogs you don't know well until his course of injections is fully complete. This will help him become well adjusted as he grows

up and less prone to being timid or fearful of the new things he will encounter. Your pup's socialization began at the breeder's but now it is your responsibility to continue it. The socialization he receives up until the age of 12 weeks is the most critical, as this is the time when he forms his impressions of the outside world. Be especially careful during the eight-to-ten-week period, also known as the fear period. The interaction he receives during this time should be gentle and reassuring. Lack of socialization can manifest itself in fear and aggression as the dog grows up. He needs lots of human contact, affection, handling and exposure to other animals.

Once your pup has received his necessary vaccinations, feel

FINANCIAL RESPONSIBILITY
Grooming tools, collars, leashes, crate, dog beds and, of course, toys will be expenses to you when you first obtain your pup, and the cost will continue throughout your dog's lifetime. If your puppy damages or destroys your possessions (as most puppies surely will!) or something belonging to a neighbor, you can calculate additional expense. There is also flea and pest control, which every dog owner faces more than once. You must be able to handle the financial responsibility of owning a dog.

59

SOCIALIZATION

Thorough socialization includes not only meeting new people but also being introduced to new experiences such as riding in the car, having his coat brushed, hearing the television, walking in a crowd—the list is endless. The more your pup experiences, and the more positive the experiences are, the less of a shock and the less scary it will be for your pup to encounter new things.

free to take him out and about (on his lead, of course). Walk him around the neighborhood, take him on your daily errands, let people pet him, let him meet other dogs and pets, etc. Puppies do not have to try to make friends; there will be no shortage of people who will want to introduce themselves. Just make sure that you carefully supervise each meeting. If the neighborhood children want to say hello, for example, that is great—children and pups most often make great companions. Sometimes an excited child can unintentionally handle a pup too roughly, or an overzealous pup can playfully nip a little too hard. You want to make socialization experiences positive ones. What a pup learns during this very formative stage will impact his attitude toward future encounters. You want your dog to be comfortable around everyone. A pup that has a bad experience with a child may grow up to be a dog that is shy around or aggressive toward children.

CONSISTENCY IN TRAINING

Dogs, being pack animals, naturally need a leader, or else they try to establish dominance in their packs. When you bring a dog into your family, the choice of who becomes the leader and who becomes the pack is entirely up to you! Your pup's intuitive quest for dominance, coupled with the fact that it is nearly impossible to look at an adorable Springer Spaniel pup, with his "puppy-dog" eyes and his floppy ears, and not cave in, give the pup almost an unfair advantage in getting the upper hand! A pup will definitely test the waters to see what he can and cannot do. Do not give in to those sad spaniel eyes—stand your ground when it comes to disciplining the pup and make sure that all family members do the same. It will only confuse the pup when Mother tells him to get off the couch when he is used to sitting up there with Father to watch the nightly news. Avoid discrepancies by having all members of the household decide on the rules before the pup even comes home...and be consistent in enforcing them! Early training shapes the dog's personality, so you cannot be unclear in what you expect.

If you don't want your Springer(s) on the furniture, enforce the rules early on. Otherwise, you may find that your favorite spot on the sofa has "gone to the dogs!"

COMMON PUPPY PROBLEMS

The best way to prevent puppy problems is to be proactive in stopping an undesirable behavior as soon as it starts. The old saying "You can't teach an old dog new tricks" does not necessarily hold true, but it is true that it is much easier to discourage bad behavior in a young developing pup than to wait until the pup's bad behavior becomes the adult dog's bad habit. There are some problems that are especially prevalent in puppies as they develop.

NIPPING

As puppies start to teethe, they feel the need to sink their teeth into anything

IN DUE TIME
It will take at least two weeks for your puppy to become accustomed to his new surroundings. Give him lots of love, attention, handling, frequent opportunities to relieve himself, a diet he likes to eat and a place he can call his own.

61

teeth grow in and his jaws develop, and he continues to think it is okay to gnaw on human appendages. Your Springer Spaniel does not mean any harm with a friendly nip,

Springers love the great outdoors, no matter the weather. This pup looks like he's enjoyed his first encounter with snow.

available...unfortunately that includes your fingers, arms, hair and toes. You may find this behavior cute for the first five seconds...until you feel just how sharp those puppy teeth are. This is something you want to discourage immediately and consistently with a firm "No!" (or whatever number of firm "No's" it takes for him to understand that you mean business). Then replace your finger with an appropriate chew toy. While this behavior is merely annoying when the dog is young, it can become highly unpleasant as your Springer Spaniel's adult

CHEWING TIPS

Chewing goes hand in hand with nipping in the sense that a teething puppy is always looking for a way to soothe his aching gums. In this case, instead of chewing on you, he may have taken a liking to your favorite shoe or something else which he should not be chewing. Again, realize that this is a normal canine behavior that does not need to be discouraged, only redirected. Your pup just needs to be taught what is acceptable to chew on and what is off-limits. Consistently tell him "No!" when you catch him chewing on something forbidden and give him a chew toy.

Conversely, praise him when you catch him chewing on something appropriate. In this way, you are discouraging the inappropriate behavior and reinforcing the desired behavior. The puppy's chewing should stop after his adult teeth have come in, but an adult dog continues to chew for various reasons—perhaps because he is bored, needs to relieve tension or just likes to chew. That is why it is important to redirect his chewing when he is still young.

but he also does not know his own strength.

CRYING/WHINING

Your pup will often cry, whine, whimper, howl or make some type of commotion when he is left alone. This is basically his way of calling out for attention to make sure that you know he is there and that you have not forgotten about him. He feels insecure when he is left alone, when you are out of the house and he is in his crate or when you are in another part of the house and he cannot see you. The noise he is making is an expression of the anxiety he feels at being alone, so he needs to be taught that being alone is okay. You are not actually training the dog to stop making noise, you are training him to feel comfortable when he is alone and thus removing the need for him to make the noise. This is where the crate with cozy bedding and a toy comes in handy. You want to know that he is safe when you are not there to supervise, and you know that he will be safe in his crate rather than roaming freely about the house. In order for the pup to stay in his crate without making a fuss, he needs to be comfortable in his crate. On that note, it is extremely important that the crate is never used as a form of punishment, or the pup will have a negative association with the crate.

Accustom the pup to the crate in short, gradually increasing time intervals in which you put him in the crate, maybe with a treat, and stay in the room with him. If he cries or makes a fuss, do not go to him, but stay in his sight. Gradually he will realize that staying in his crate is okay without your help, and it will not be so traumatic for him when you are not around. You may want to leave the radio on softly when you leave the house; the sound of human voices may be comforting to him.

Whether you intend to hunt with your Springer or just enjoy him as a pet, the English Springer Spaniel makes a wonderful companion for the right owners.

DIETARY AND FEEDING CONSIDERATIONS

Today the choices of food for your English Springer Spaniel are many and varied. There are simply dozens of brands of food in all sorts of flavors and textures, ranging from puppy diets to those for seniors. There are even hypoallergenic and low-calorie diets available. Because your English Springer Spaniel's food has a bearing on coat, health and temperament, it is essential that the most suitable diet be selected for a dog of his age. It is fair to say, however, that even dedicated owners can be somewhat perplexed by the enormous range of foods available. Only understanding what is best for your dog will help you reach a valued decision.

There are four basic types of dog foods: fresh, preferably raw meat; dry food; semi-moist food; and canned meat. For meat the most commonly used is tripe, and dogs love it. You can combine their meat meals with dry food or with a semi-moist meal or, if fresh meat is not available, with canned meat. Dry foods are useful for the cost-conscious for overall they tend to be less expensive than semi-moist or canned, but dogs often get bored with them. How would you feel if you had the same meal day after day, year after year? Dry food contains the least fat and the most preservatives. In general, canned foods are made

FOOD PREFERENCE

Selecting the best dry dog food is difficult. There is no majority consensus among veterinary scientists as to the value of nutrient analysis (protein, fat, fiber, moisture, ash, cholesterol, minerals, etc.). All agree that feeding trials are what matter, but you also have to consider the individual dog. The dog's weight, age and activity level, and what pleases his taste, all must be considered. It is probably best to take the advice of your veterinarian. Every dog's dietary requirements vary, even during the lifetime of a particular dog.

If your dog is fed a good dry food, it does not require supplements of meat or vegetables. Dogs do appreciate a little variety in their diets, so you may choose to stay with the same brand but vary the flavor. Alternatively, you may wish to add a little flavored stock to give a difference to the taste.

A well-balanced puppy food will provide your young Springer with the nutrition he needs to grow up healthy.

up of 60–70% water, while semi-moist ones often contain so much sugar that they are perhaps the least preferred by owners, even though their dogs seem to like

TEST FOR PROPER DIET
A good test for proper diet is the color, odor and firmness of your dog's stool. A healthy dog usually produces three semi-hard stools per day. The stools should have no unpleasant odor. They should be the same color from excretion to excretion.

them. Most dogs love vegetables and fruit and it certainly doesn't do them any harm to surprise them with a quarter of an apple, some leftover green beans or lettuce.

When selecting your dog's diet, three stages of development must be considered: the puppy stage, the adult stage and the senior stage.

PUPPY DIETS
Puppies instinctively want to suck milk from their dam's teats and a normal puppy will exhibit

65

usually every two hours during the first few days of life.

Puppies should be allowed to nurse from their dam for about the first six weeks, although from the third or fourth week the breeder will have begun to introduce small portions of suitable solid food. Most breeders like to introduce alternate milk and meat meals initially, building up to weaning time.

By the time the puppies are seven or a maximum of eight weeks old, they should be fully weaned and fed solely on a

The breeder introduces the litter to solid food between the third and fourth week.

this behavior from just a few moments following birth. If puppies do not attempt to suckle within the first half-hour or so, they should be encouraged to do so by placing them on the nipples, having selected ones with plenty of milk. This early milk supply is important in providing colostrum to protect the puppies during the first eight to ten weeks of their lives. Although a dam's milk is much better than any milk formula, despite there being some excellent ones available, if the puppies do not feed you will have to feed them yourself. For those with less experience, advice from a veterinarian is important so that you feed not only the right quantity of milk but that of correct quality, fed at suitably frequent intervals,

FEEDING TIPS
• Dog food must be served at room temperature, neither too hot nor too cold. Fresh water, changed daily and served in a clean bowl, is mandatory, especially when feeding dry food.
• Never feed your dog from the table while you are eating, and never feed your dog leftovers from your own meal. They usually contain too much fat and too much seasoning.
• Dogs must chew their food. Hard pellets are excellent; soups and stews are to be avoided.
• Don't add leftovers or any extras to commercial dog food. The normal food is usually balanced, and adding something extra destroys the balance.
• Except for age-related changes, dogs do not require dietary variations. They can be fed the same diet, day after day, without becoming bored or ill.

This Springer litter is certainly keeping mother busy! Their dam's milk is critical and necessary for the pups for their first six weeks.

proprietary puppy food. Selection of the most suitable, good-quality diet at this time is essential for a puppy's fastest growth rate is during the first year of life. Veterinarians are usually able to offer advice in this regard and, although the frequency of meals will have been reduced over time, only when a young dog has reached the age of about 18 months should an adult diet be fed.

Puppy and junior diets should be well balanced for the needs of your dog, so that except in certain circumstances additional vitamins, minerals and proteins will not be required.

When you decided to buy your puppy, the breeder probably told you what you have to feed

STORING DOG FOOD
You must store your dry dog food carefully. Open packages of dog food quickly lose their vitamin value, usually within 90 days of being opened. Mold spores and vermin could also contaminate the food.

67

the puppy once you bring him home. This is important for two reasons: coming to live with his new owners in totally new surroundings is already a stressful experience for the puppy and a continuation of his diet will help him. Even then, his tummy may be upset the first couple of days, or he may even refuse to eat for a day or two, but don't worry about that. As soon as he is settled down he will eat again, especially if it's the food he has been used to. Also, the breeder most likely has a lot of experience in feeding mature dogs and puppies and keeping them in a peak condition, so it would be wise to listen to his advice. Most breeders will provide you with an exact list of what to feed the puppy at which stage of

his life and we strongly advise you to follow these instructions. Once your puppy is a mature one or two year old, you can change his diet to what is more convenient for you (availability, costs, etc.), but with the growing puppy and youngster, stay with the breeder's diet. And remember that if ten breeders are discussing the feeding of their dogs, you will hear ten different opinions, and all of them will be right!

Your puppy will need three or four meals a day until he is about nine months old, then you can cut back to two daily meals. Some people prefer to feed the adult dog once a day but if your dog loves his food, he probably won't go along with that! He might prefer to have a breakfast and a dinner.

GRAIN-BASED DIETS

Some less expensive dog foods are based on grains and other plant proteins. While these products may appear to be attractively priced, many breeders prefer a diet based on animal proteins and believe that they are more conducive to your dog's health. Many grain-based diets rely on soy protein, which may cause flatulence (passing gas).

There are many cases, however, when your dog might require a special diet. These special requirements should only be recommended by your veterinarian.

ADULT DIETS

A dog is considered an adult when he has stopped growing. The growth is in height and/or length. Do not consider the dog's weight when the decision is made to switch from a puppy diet to a maintenance diet. Again you should rely on your breeder's advice. A Springer Spaniel reaches adulthood at about two years of age, though some dogs are fully mature at 18 months while others may take up to three years.

Major dog-food manufacturers specialize in maintenance diets, and it is just necessary for you to

these changes take place slowly, they might not be recognizable. What is easily recognizable is weight gain. By continuing to feed your dog an adult-maintenance diet when he is slowing down metabolically, your dog will gain weight. Obesity in an older dog compounds the health problems that already accompany old age. So here as well, feed "with your eyes."

As your dog gets older, few of their organs function up to par. The kidneys slow down and the intestines become less efficient. These age-related factors are best handled with a change in diet and a change in feeding schedule to give smaller portions that are more easily digested.

There is no single best diet for every older dog. While many dogs do well on light or senior diets, other dogs do better on puppy diets or other special premium diets such as lamb and rice. Be sensitive to your senior English Springer Spaniel's diet and this will help control other problems that may arise with your old friend.

Once your Springer stops growing, he can begin an adult maintenance diet. A nutritionally complete adult diet will likely suffice for the rest of the dog's life unless otherwise indicated by the vet.

select the one best suited to your dog's needs. Whatever you are going to feed your dog, don't rely entirely on the quantities given in the manufacturer's instructions. Every dog has different requirements, active dogs may have different requirements than sedate dogs and—as in humans—where one dog will grow fat on just a small portion, another will need to double the quantity. So it is best to "feed with your eyes'"

SENIOR DIETS

As dogs get older, their metabolism changes. The older dog usually exercises less, moves more slowly and sleeps more. This change in lifestyle and physiological performance requires a change in diet. Since

WATER

Just as your dog needs proper nutrition from his food, water is an essential "nutrient" as well. Water keeps the dog's body properly hydrated and promotes normal function of the body's systems. During housebreaking, it

Sporting dogs, bred to run and hunt for a whole day, have much energy to expend on a daily basis. Exercise is a vital component in your Springer's schedule.

is necessary to keep an eye on how much water your English Springer Spaniel is drinking, but once he is reliably trained he should have access to clean fresh water at all times. Make sure that the dog's water bowl is clean, and change the water often, making sure that water is always available for your dog, especially if you feed dry food.

You will find that your Springer Spaniel is a very sloppy drinker: he loves his water bowl and in his enthusiasm he will often put not only his mouth but also both front paws in the bowl. Or he will take one last mouthful of water and before swallowing it come to you to tell you how much he loves you! A special spaniel bowl may help you keep the kitchen floor clean.

EXERCISE

All dogs require some form of exercise, regardless of breed. A sedentary lifestyle is as harmful to a dog as it is to a person. The Springer Spaniel is a very lively and active breed that requires a lot of free exercise. He might like to come with you on a shopping expedition but what he needs is to run around free, preferably in exciting surroundings, like woods or fields, where he can develop his hunting instincts.

Owners often make mistakes in the exercise they give their dog. Whereas the new puppy is

an exciting thing, they tend to give too much exercise. It is only human to show off with something you are very proud of, but it means that the small puppy is taken on too many walks. For a puppy up to six months, the yard is big enough. Provided he is properly inoculated, take him to the park once a day to let him socialize and play with the other dogs for about 15 minutes. Once the puppy is about nine months old, you can extend the daily walks to an hour daily and once he is a year old his energy will be boundless.

We cannot stress the importance of exercise enough. It is essential to keep the dog's body fit, but it is also essential to his mental well being. A bored dog will find something to do, which often manifests itself in some type of destructive behavior. In this sense, it is essential for your mental well being as well!

GROOMING
BRUSHING

A natural bristle brush or a slicker brush can be used for regular routine brushing. Daily brushing is effective for removing dead hair and stimulating the dog's natural oils to add shine and a healthy look to the coat. Also, the soft and silky spaniel

coat can easily form tangles and mats, especially in places like the armpits and behind the ears and it is important to prevent these from forming.

TRIMMING AND PRESENTATION

When you buy your puppy, he will have a smooth, short coat without much feathering, but by the time your puppy is five or six months old, you'll find that fluffy puppy hair starts growing on his head and throat, his feet and his legs and on his markings. Your

dog will have lost his shiny coat but don't worry, this doesn't mean he is not healthy! It is just his puppy coat, which he will grow out of in due time.

The English Springer Spaniel's coat is flat, straight and silky. The best way to shape the coat is by hand-plucking. You may prefer using thumblettes, which fit over the thumb and forefinger, or surgical gloves to get a better grip but resist the temptation of using the thinning scissors as long as possible. Clipping and razoring are absolutely out of the question since they destroy the density of color and you will never get that lovely, silky sheen that you get when you handtrim the coat.

The Springer requires regular brushing to keep his coat neat and mat-free.

GROOMING EQUIPMENT

How much grooming equipment you purchase will depend on how much grooming you are going to do. Here are some basics:

- Natural bristle brush
- Slicker brush
- Metal comb
- Scissors
- Blow dryer
- Rubber mat
- Dog shampoo
- Spray hose attachment
- Ear cleaner
- Cotton balls
- Towels
- Nail clippers

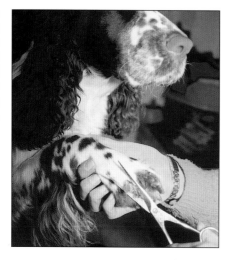

If you think you are not up to this job, you'll have to seek help. Ask the breeder whether he can help you. Some breeders use their (little) spare time to trim. If not, you'll have to take your puppy to a professional groomer. Be very careful where you go, since some grooming parlors often believe that their canine clients want nothing but having all of their "excess hair" removed. For the lovely Springer, that means that the featherings on his legs go, his back is clippered and the beautiful feathering on the ears is cut off. You have to stress the fact that what you want is a show trim. Your Springer must be shaped in the model in which he looks his best and, again, this should be done by hand-plucking and not by scissoring or clippering.

The puppy's coat may take some time to get ready to come out; sometimes you have to wait until the puppy is eight or nine months old. This can be annoying when you want to show the puppy, but be patient! Don't hurry the coat by using cutting instruments; you will regret that later.

What you should do in the meantime is groom your puppy regularly so that he is quite used to being on a table and being handled. Also the abundant hair around the feet, between the pads on the underside and at the inside of the ear around the ear opening can be cut away.

When you find that your puppy's coat is ready to come out, you may find it easier to remove the hair by using thumblettes or thin surgical gloves, which are quite tight fitting.

Other equipment you may need includes a fine-toothed metal comb with short teeth (or a flea comb), a wider toothed long-bladed comb, a pair of scissors as used by a hairdresser, a pair of thinning scissors with one normal blade and one blade with fine teeth, and a trimming blade.

Start with the head. Gently pull out the long hair on top of the skull, always pulling in the direction the hair grows. This sounds painful, but it is not, since what you pull out is dead hair. Start with just a couple of hairs so that your puppy can get used to the feel and you won't run the risk of hurting him by pulling out too many hairs at the same time. If you have a really smooth finish

Your Springer's teeth need attention, too. Pet shops will sell toothbrushes and toothpaste made especially for dogs.

on top of the head, go to the top of the ears and remove the long hairs there, shaping around the back of the ear and about one-third on the way down. You might use the trimming blade here if you cannot manage with the thumblettes.

With your thinning scissors, cut carefully under the corner of the ear next to the head and the inside of the ear. Vets will often tell you that spaniels always have ear problems. This is not true. As long as you keep the inside of the ear clean and free of hair so that the ear can "breathe" and, if necessary, use ear cleaner, you'll find that your Springer's ears do not have problems.

Next, thin out all the long and surplus hair from the breastbone up to and including the throat. Don't forget the underside of the lower jaw and the inside of the lipfolds. Make the hair very short here.

The neck must be trimmed out as short as possible, also with finger and thumb. If you have

Rubber thumblettes are used to pluck hairs that are starting to molt.

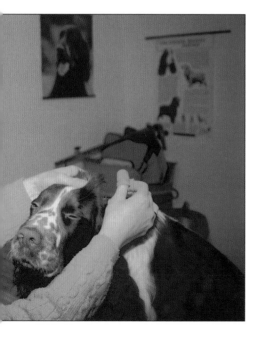

73

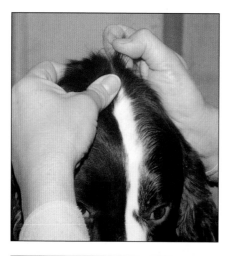

Scenes from a grooming session: (top) hand plucking, (middle) trimming hair on the ears and (bottom) using a fine-toothed comb.

used the fine comb regularly, you'll find that it will have removed nearly all the puppy fluff. Try to use the comb as a stripper by gripping the hair between the comb and your thumb and pulling it towards you. It helps when you weave an elastic band between the teeth of the comb. Make a smooth transition from throat and chest to shoulder blades with the thinning scissors.

Continue down the shoulders until they are smooth and clear. The forelegs may have some fluffy hair on the sides and the front. This must be removed. The feathering at the backside of the front legs stays as it is. The feathering should not touch the ground; when it does, you can shape it with the scissors. When viewed from the front, the feathering should lie backwards quite naturally from the elbow.

Work the comb with the elastic band through the body coat, the hair on the ribs and on the outside of the hindlegs. Pluck the fluffy hair that won't come out with the comb. Leave the feathering on the front and back but remove the fluffy hair on the side. Shape the hair on the hock with the thinning scissors.

Trim the tail and cut underneath it. Pluck the hair down to where the feathering falls downwards and trim the feathering into shape.

Trimming the feet is not easy and you have to be very careful. Start with lifting the foot and cutting out all the surplus hair from underneath. Cut closely around the outline of the foot. Then put the foot down and cut the surplus hair away that sticks up between the toes with the thinning scissors. Cut in the direction of the toes. Do not cut the hair between the toes away, since that makes the foot look like a splayed foot. Finish off with a good brush and your Springer is now a picture of health and condition.

BATHING

Dogs do not need to be bathed as often as humans, but sometimes a bath will be necessary. It is therefore important that you accustom your pup to being bathed as a puppy, so that he is used to it when he grows up. You will have to bathe your dog the day before a show and most owners like to bathe their bitches after they have been in season.

Before you bathe your dog, check the coat for tangles. Make sure that your dog has a good non-slip surface to stand on. Begin by wetting the dog's coat. A shower or hose attachment is necessary for thoroughly wetting and rinsing the coat. Check the water temperature to make sure that it is neither too hot nor too cold. Fill his ear openings with a piece of cotton so that there is no

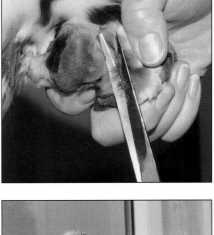

Scenes from a grooming session: (top) trimming the tail, (middle) trimming hair between the foot pads and (bottom) trimming hair on the muzzle.

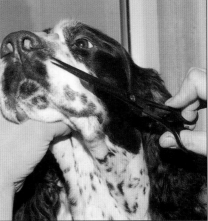

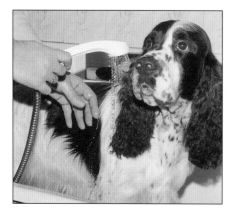

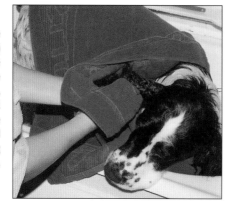

Bathing the Springer: (top) thoroughly wet the coat before shampooing, (middle) towel drying to remove excess water and (bottom) finishing with a blow dryer.

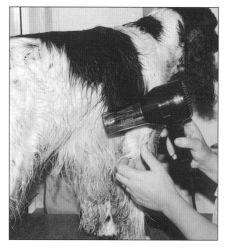

chance of water or soap getting into the ear canals. (Don't forget to remove it after the bath.)

Next, apply shampoo to the dog's coat and work it into a good lather. You should purchase a shampoo that is made for dogs; do not use a product made for human hair. Wash the head last; you do not want shampoo to drip into the dog's eyes while you are washing the rest of his body. Work the shampoo all the way down to the skin. You can use this opportunity to check the skin for any bumps, bites or other abnormalities. Do not neglect any area of the body—get all of the hard-to-reach places.

Once the dog has been thoroughly shampooed, he requires an equally thorough rinsing. Shampoo left in the coat can become irritating to the skin. Protect his eyes from the shampoo by

SOAP IT UP

The use of human soap products like shampoo, bubble bath and hand soap can be damaging to a dog's coat and skin. Human products are too strong; they remove the protective oils coating the dog's hair and skin that make him water-resistant. Use only shampoo made especially for dogs. You may like to use a medicated shampoo, which will help to keep external parasites at bay.

shielding them with your hand and directing the flow of water in the opposite direction.

Be prepared for your dog to shake out his coat—you might want to stand back, but make sure you have a hold on the dog to keep him from running through the house.

EAR CLEANING

The ears should be kept clean and any excess hair inside the ear should be trimmed. Ears can be cleaned with wipes made especially for dogs and especially for this purpose. Be on the lookout for any signs of infections or ear-mite infestation and during the summer for grass seeds that may be picked up from the grass by the

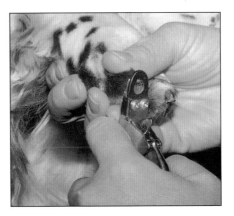

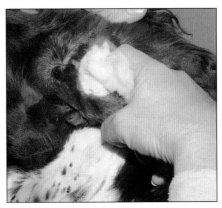

(Top) Trimming nails with a guillotine-type clipper, (middle) cleaning ears and (bottom) scaling teeth, which is usually done by the vet.

BATHING BEAUTY

Once you are sure that the dog is thoroughly rinsed, squeeze the excess water out of his coat with your hand and dry him with a heavy towel. You may choose to use a blow dryer on his coat or just let it dry naturally. In cold weather, never allow your dog outside with a wet coat.

There are "dry bath" products on the market, which are sprays and powders intended for spot cleaning, that can be used between regular baths if necessary. They are not substitutes for regular baths, but they are easy to use for touch-ups as they do not require rinsing.

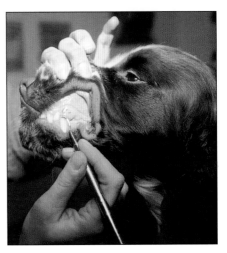

ears and find their way into the ear canal. If your English Springer Spaniel has been shaking his head or scratching at his ears frequently, this usually indicates a problem. Don't clean the ear canal yourself. If you poke into the ear canal with tweezers or a cotton swab, you'll only succeed in aggravating things. Contact your vet before the condition gets serious. If his ears have an unusual odor, this is a sure sign of mite infestation or infection, and a signal to have his ears checked by the veterinarian.

If you check your spaniel's ears regularly and use the ear wipes when the ear doesn't look 100% clean, you will find that the spaniel's reputation for ear-trouble is totally unfounded.

NAIL CLIPPING

Your Springer should be accustomed to having his nails trimmed at an early age, since it will be a part of your maintenance routine throughout his life. Not only does it look nicer but a dog with long nails can cause injury if he jumps up or if he scratches someone unintentionally. Also, a long nail has a better chance of ripping and bleeding, or causing feet to spread. A good rule of thumb is that if you can hear your dog's nails clicking on the floor when he walks, his nails are too long.

Before you start cutting make sure you can identify the "quick"

in each nail. The quick is a blood vessel that runs through the center of each nail and grows rather close to the end. It will bleed profusely if accidentally cut, which will be quite painful for the dog as it contains nerve endings. Keep some type of clotting agent on hand, such as a styptic pencil or styptic powder (the type used for shaving). This will stop the bleeding quickly when applied to the end of the cut nail. Do not panic if this happens, just stop the bleeding and talk soothingly to your dog. Once he has calmed down, move on to the next nail. It is better to clip a little at a time, particularly with black-nailed dogs.

Hold your pup steady as you begin trimming his nails; you do not want him to make any

PEDICURE TIP

A dog that spends a lot of time outside on a hard surface, such as cement or pavement, will have his nails naturally worn down and may not need to have them trimmed as often, except maybe in the colder months when he is not outside as much. Regardless, it is best to get your dog accustomed to the nail-trimming procedure at an early age so that he is used to it. Some dogs are especially sensitive about having their feet touched, but if a dog has experienced it since puppyhood, it should not bother him.

sudden movements or jump off the table. Talk to him soothingly and stroke his coat as you clip. Holding his foot in your hand, simply take off the end of each nail in one quick clip. You can purchase nail clippers that are specially made for dogs; you can probably find them wherever you buy pet supplies. You may find the guillotine type the best ones to use.

If you feel all this is beyond you, you might prefer the use of a nail grinder. This is a small battery-operated appliance that slowly grinds the nails. There is no fear of cutting into the quick and most dogs don't mind the buzzing sound of the grinder at all.

TRAVELING WITH YOUR DOG
CAR TRAVEL
You should accustom your English Springer Spaniel to riding in a car at an early age. If you are lucky, the breeder has already taken the puppies in his car for a visit to the vet or just for a ride, so that when you come to take your puppy home he knows what it is to be in a car. You will find that most Springers love to ride in the car.

The best way for a dog to travel in a car is in his crate. You can use either the fiberglass or the wire crates. Another option is the specially made safety harness for dogs, which straps the dog in

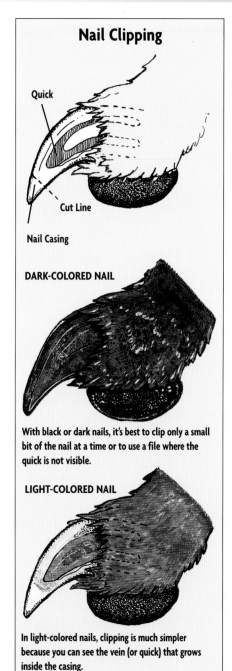

Nail Clipping

Quick

Cut Line

Nail Casing

DARK-COLORED NAIL

With black or dark nails, it's best to clip only a small bit of the nail at a time or to use a file where the quick is not visible.

LIGHT-COLORED NAIL

In light-colored nails, clipping is much simpler because you can see the vein (or quick) that grows inside the casing.

Your local pet shop will have a large supply of grooming tools that you can use on your English Springer Spaniel.

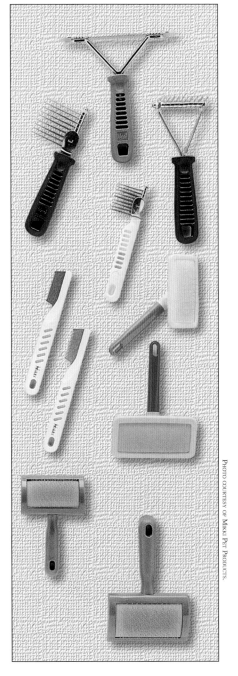

PHOTO COURTESY OF MIKKI PET PRODUCTS.

much like a seat belt. Do not let the dog roam loose in the vehicle—this is very dangerous! If you should stop short, your dog can be thrown and injured. If the dog starts climbing on you and pestering you while you are driving, you will not be able to concentrate on the road. It is an unsafe situation for everyone—human and canine.

The best way to accustom your puppy to traveling in the car is by doing it gradually. Start with putting the puppy in the crate, while you sit behind the steering wheel. Talk to him and tell him how much he will enjoy this. Repeat this the next day and start the car, let the engine run for a couple of minutes. The day after that drive around the block and gradually extend your trips. Drive to the park and let him have a quick run and feed him when you come home. Whatever you do, make it fun for him.

For long trips, be prepared to stop to let the dog relieve himself.

TOO HOT TO HANDLE

Never leave your dog alone in the car. In hot weather your dog can die from the high temperature inside a closed vehicle; even a car parked in the shade can heat up very quickly. Leaving the window open is dangerous as well since the dog can hurt himself trying to get out.

Bring along whatever you need to clean up after him. You should bring along some paper towels, should he have an accident in the car or despite your preparations become carsick.

AIR TRAVEL

Contact your chosen airline before proceeding with your travel plans that include your Springer. The dog will be required to travel in a fiberglass crate and you should always check in advance with the airline regarding specific requirements for the crate's size, type and labeling. To help put the dog at ease, give him one of his favorite toys in the crate. Do not feed the dog for several hours prior to checking in so that you minimize his need to relieve himself. However, some airlines require that the dog must be fed within four hours of arriving at the airport, in which case a light meal is best. For long trips, you will have to attach food and water bowls to the dog's crate so that airline employees can tend to him between legs of the trip.

Make sure your dog is properly identified and that your contact information appears on his ID tags and on his crate. Animals travel in a different area of the plane than human passengers so every rule must be strictly adhered to so as to prevent the risk of getting separated from your dog.

ON THE ROAD

If you are going on a long motor trip with your dog, be sure the hotels are dog-friendly. Many hotels do not accept dogs. Also take along some ice that can be thawed and offered to your dog if he becomes overheated. Most dogs like to lick ice.

BOARDING

So you want to take a family vacation—and you want to include *all* members of your family. You would probably make arrangements for accommodations ahead of time anyway, but this is especially important when traveling with a dog. You do not want to make an overnight stop at the only place around for miles to find out that they do not allow dogs. Also, you do not want to reserve a place for your family without mentioning that you are bringing a dog, because if it is against their policy you may not have a place to stay.

The most acceptable, safest way of traveling with your English Springer Spaniel in a car is in a crate. It is dangerous for the dog to have free access to all parts of the vehicle while it is moving.

by to see the facility and where the dogs are kept to make sure that it is clean. Talk to the owner or the manager and see how he treats the dogs—do they spend time with the dogs, play with them, exercise them, etc.? You know that your Springer will not be happy unless he gets regular activity. Also find out the kennel's policy on vaccinations and what they require. This is for all of the dogs' safety, since when dogs are kept together, there is a greater risk of diseases being passed from dog to dog.

IDENTIFICATION

Your Springer is your valued companion and friend. That is why you always keep a close eye on him and you have made sure that he cannot escape from the yard or wriggle out of his collar and run away from you. However, accidents can happen and there may come a time when your dog unexpectedly gets separated from you. If this unfortunate event

No dogs travel as much as show dogs. Dog shows take place on every weekend of the year all across the country.

Alternatively, if you are traveling and choose not to bring your Springer, you will have to make arrangements for him while you are away. Some options are to bring him to a neighbor's house to stay while you are away, to have a trusted neighbor stop by often or stay at your house, or bring your dog to a reputable boarding kennel. If you choose to board him at a kennel, you should stop

EXERCISE ALERT!
You should be careful where you exercise your dog. Many areas have been sprayed with chemicals that are highly toxic to both dogs and humans. Never allow your dog to eat grass or drink from puddles on either public or private grounds, as the run-off water may contain chemicals from sprays and herbicides.

IDENTIFICATION OPTIONS

As puppies become more and more expensive, especially those puppies of high quality for showing and/or breeding, they have a greater chance of being stolen. The usual collar dog tag is, of course, easily removed. But there are two more permanent techniques that have become widely used for identification.

The puppy microchip implantation involves the injection of a small microchip, about the size of a corn kernel, under the skin of the dog. If your dog shows up at a clinic or shelter, or is offered for resale under less-than-savory circumstances, it can be positively identified by the microchip. The microchip is scanned, and a registry quickly identifies you as the owner.

Tattooing is done on various parts of the dog, from his belly to his cheeks. The number tattooed can be your telephone number or any other number that you can easily memorize. When professional dog thieves see a tattooed dog, they usually lose interest. Both microchipping and tattooing can be done at your local veterinary clinic. For the safety of our dogs, no laboratory facility or dog broker will accept a tattooed dog as stock.

Discuss microchipping and tattooing with your veterinarian and breeder. Some vets perform these services on their own premises for a reasonable fee. Be certain that the dog do is then properly registered with a legitimate national database.

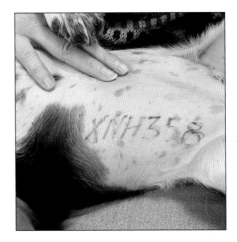

Tattooing for identification. This Springer has his ID number tattooed clearly across his belly.

should occur, the first thing on your mind will be finding him. Proper identification will increase the chances of his being returned to you safely and quickly. Tattooing or microchipping the puppies before they leave the breeder is common practice. This is often done by the American Kennel Club so that the number that is given to the puppy either as an earmark or via the microchip is unique and can also be recorded on his pedigree.

ID tags are the traditional way of identifying your dog. Your Springer should have his tags securely fastened to his collar, which should be worn at all times.

83

Training Your
ENGLISH SPRINGER SPANIEL

Living with an untrained dog is a lot like owning a piano that you do not know how to play—it is a nice object to look at but it does not do much more than that to bring you pleasure. Now try taking piano lessons and suddenly the piano comes alive and brings forth magical sounds and rhythms that set your heart singing and your body swaying.

The same is true with your English Springer Spaniel. Any dog is a big responsibility and if not trained sensibly may develop unacceptable behavior that annoys you or could even cause family friction.

To train your Springer, you may like to enroll in an obedience class. Teach him good manners as you learn how and why he behaves the way he does. Find out how to communicate with your dog and how to recognize and understand his communications with you. Suddenly the dog takes on a new role in your life—he is clever, interesting, well behaved and fun to be with. He demonstrates his bond of devotion to you daily. In other words, your English Springer Spaniel does wonders for your ego because he constantly reminds you that you are not only his leader, you are his hero!

Those involved with teaching dog obedience and counseling owners about their dogs' behavior have discovered some interesting facts about dog ownership. For example, training dogs when they are puppies results in the highest rate of success in developing well-mannered and well-adjusted adult dogs. Training an older dog, from six months to six years of age, can produce almost equal results providing that the owner accepts the dog's slower rate of learning capability and is willing to work patiently to help the dog succeed at developing to his fullest potential. Unfortunately, many owners of untrained adult dogs lack the patience factor, so they do not

HONOR AND OBEY
Dogs are the most honorable animals in existence. They consider another species (humans) as their own. They interface with you. You are their leader. Puppies perceive children to be on their level; their actions around small children are different from their behavior around their adult masters.

All members of the family should take part in training the puppy. Your Springer should grow up to obey commands no matter who issues them.

water, shelter and security. He latches onto you and wants to stay close. He will usually follow you from room to room, will not let you out of his sight when you are outdoors with him, and respond in like manner to the people and animals you encounter. If you greet a friend warmly, he will be happy to greet the person as well. If, however, you are hesitant, even anxious, about the approach of a stranger, he will respond accordingly.

Once the puppy begins to produce hormones, his natural curiosity emerges and he begins to investigate the world around him. It is at this time when you may notice that the untrained dog begins to wander away from you and even ignore your commands to stay close.

There are usually classes within a reasonable distance of the owner's home, but you also do a lot to train your dog yourself. Sometimes there are classes avail-

persist until their dogs are successful at learning particular behaviors.

Training a puppy, aged 10 to 16 weeks (20 weeks at the most), is like working with a dry sponge in a pool of water. The pup soaks up whatever you show him and constantly looks for more things to do and learn. At this early age, his body is not yet producing hormones, and therein lies the reason for such a high rate of success. Without hormones, he is focused on his owners and not particularly interested in investigating other places, dogs, people, etc. You are his leader: his provider of food,

---

THINK BEFORE YOU BARK
Dogs are sensitive to their masters' moods and emotions. Use your voice wisely when communicating with your dog. Never raise your voice at your dog unless you are trying to correct him. "Barking" at your dog can become as meaningless as "dogspeak" is to you.

able but the tuition is too costly. Whatever the circumstances, the solution to training your Springer without formal obedience classes lies within the pages of this book.

This chapter is devoted to helping you train your English Springer Spaniel at home. If the recommended procedures are followed faithfully, you may expect positive results that will prove rewarding to both you and your dog.

Whether your new charge is a puppy or a mature adult, the methods of teaching and the techniques we use in training basic behaviors are the same. After all, no dog, whether puppy or adult, likes harsh or inhumane methods. All creatures, however, respond favorably to gentle motivational methods and sincere praise and encouragement. Now let us get started.

PARENTAL GUIDANCE

Training a dog is a life experience. Many parents admit that much of what they know about raising children they learned from caring for their dogs. Dogs respond to love, fairness and guidance, just as children do. Become a good dog owner and you may become an even better parent.

HOUSEBREAKING

You can train a puppy to relieve itself wherever you choose, but this must be somewhere suitable. You should bear in mind from the outset that when your puppy is old enough to go out in public places, any canine deposits must be removed at once. You will always have to carry with you a small plastic bag or "poop-scoop."

Outdoor training includes such surfaces as grass, soil and cement. Indoor training usually means training your dog to newspaper. When deciding on the surface and location that you will want your English Springer Spaniel to use, be sure it is going to be permanent. Training your dog to grass and then changing your mind two months later is extremely difficult for both dog and owner.

Next, choose the command you will use each and every time you want your puppy to void. "Hurry up" and "Potty" are examples of commands commonly used by dog owners.

Get in the habit of giving the puppy your chosen relief command before you take him out. That way, when he becomes an adult, you will be able to determine if he wants to go out when you ask him. A confirmation will be signs of interest, such as wagging his tail, watching you intently, going to the door, etc.

PUPPY'S NEEDS

The puppy needs to relieve himself after play periods, after each meal, after he has been sleeping and any time he indicates that he is looking for a place to urinate or defecate. The urinary and intestinal tract muscles of very young puppies are not fully developed. Therefore, like human babies, puppies need to relieve themselves frequently.

Take your puppy out often—every hour for an eight-week-old, for example, and always immediately after sleeping and eating. The older the puppy, the less often he will need to relieve himself. Finally, as a mature healthy adult, he will require only three to five relief trips per day.

HOUSING

Since the types of housing and control you provide for your puppy have a direct relationship

Making your Springer sit politely before he is fed reinforces that you are the one who is in charge.

HOW MANY TIMES A DAY?

AGE	RELIEF TRIPS
To 14 weeks	10
14–22 weeks	8
22–32 weeks	6
Adulthood	4
(dog stops growing)	

These are estimates, of course, but they are a guide to the *minimum* number of opportunities a dog should have each day to relieve himself.

on the success of house-training, we consider the various aspects of both before we begin training.

Bringing a new puppy home and turning him loose in your house can be compared to turning a child loose in a sports arena and telling the child that the place is all his! The sheer enormity of the place would be too much for him to handle.

87

Take advantage of your Springer's keen nose. Offer the puppy rewards for paying attention, in the form of treats and good-smelling toys.

Instead, offer the puppy clearly defined areas where he can play, sleep, eat and live. A room of the house where the family gathers is the most obvious choice. Puppies are social animals and need to feel a part of the pack right from the start. Hearing your voice, watching you while you are doing things and smelling you nearby are all positive reinforcers that he is now a member of your pack. Usually a family room, the kitchen or a nearby adjoining breakfast area is ideal for providing safety and security for both puppy and owner.

Within that room, there should be a smaller area which the puppy can call his own. An alcove, a wire or fiberglass dog crate or a fenced (not boarded!)

TRAINING RULES

If you want to be successful in training your dog, you have four rules to obey yourself:

1. Develop an understanding of how a dog thinks.
2. Do not blame the dog for lack of communication.
3. Define your dog's personality and act accordingly.
4. Have patience and be consistent.

THE SUCCESS METHOD
6 Steps to Successful Crate Training

1 Tell the puppy "Crate time!" and place him in the crate with a small treat (a piece of cheese or half of a biscuit). Let him stay in the crate for five minutes while you are in the same room. Then release him and praise lavishly. Never release him when he is fussing. Wait until he is quiet before you let him out.

2 Repeat Step 1 several times a day.

3 The next day, place the puppy in the crate as before. Let him stay there for ten minutes. Do this several times.

4 Continue building time in five-minute increments until the puppy stays in his crate for 30 minutes with you in the

room. Always take him to his relief area after prolonged periods in his crate.

5 Now go back to Step 1 and let the puppy stay in his crate for five minutes, this time while you are out of the room.

6 Once again, build crate time in five-minute increments with you out of the room. When the puppy will stay willingly in his crate (he may even fall asleep!) for 30 minutes with you out of the room, he will be ready to stay in it for several hours at a time.

corner from which he can view the activities of his new family will be fine. The size of the area or crate is the key factor here. The area must be large enough for the puppy to lie down and stretch out as well as stand up without rubbing his head on the top, yet small enough so that he cannot relieve himself at one end and sleep at the other without coming into contact with his droppings until fully trained to relieve himself outside.

Dogs are, by nature, clean animals and will not remain close to their relief areas unless forced

to do so. In those cases, they then become dirty dogs and usually remain that way for life.

The designated area should be lined with clean bedding and a toy. Water must always be available to your puppy, though it is inadvisable to provide water while the pup is crated. This will only make housebreaking that much more difficult for the puppy and you.

CONTROL
By *control*, we mean helping the puppy to create a lifestyle pattern that will be compatible to that of his human pack (you!). Just as we

guide little children to learn our way of life, we must show the puppy when it is time to play, eat, sleep, exercise and even entertain himself.

Your puppy should always sleep in his crate. He should also learn that, during times of household confusion and excessive human activity such as at breakfast when family members are preparing for the day, he can play by himself in relative safety and comfort in his designated area. Each time you leave the puppy alone, he should understand exactly where he is to stay. You can gradually increase the time he is left alone to get him used to it.

Puppies are chewers. They cannot tell the difference between dog bones, lamp cords, television wires, shoes, table legs, etc. Chewing into a television wire, for example, can be fatal to the puppy while a shorted wire can start a fire in the house. The crate keeps the pup safe and out of trouble.

THE GOLDEN RULE
The golden rule of dog training is simple. For each "question" (command), there is only one correct answer (reaction). One command = one reaction. Keep practicing the command until the dog reacts correctly without hesitating. Be repetitive but not monotonous. Dogs get bored just as people do!

If the puppy chews on the arm of the chair when he is alone, you will probably discipline him angrily when you get home. Thus, he makes the association that your coming home means he is going to be punished. (He will not remember chewing the chair and is incapable of making the association of the discipline with his naughty deed.)

Other times of excitement, such as family parties, visits, etc., can be fun for the puppy providing he can view the activities from the security of his crate or designated area. He is not underfoot and he is not being fed all sorts of tidbits that will probably cause him stomach distress, yet he still feels a part of the fun.

SCHEDULE
A puppy should be taken to his relief area each time he is released from his designated area, after meals, after a play session, when he first awakens in the morning (at age eight weeks, this can mean 5 a.m.). The puppy will indicate that he's ready "to go" by circling or sniffing busily—do not misinterpret these signs. For a puppy less than ten weeks of age, a routine of taking him out every hour is necessary. As the puppy grows, he will be able to wait for longer periods of time.

Keep trips to his relief area short. Stay no more than five or six minutes and then return to the

Canine Development Schedule

It is important to understand how and at what age a puppy develops into adulthood. If you are a puppy owner, consult the following Canine Development Schedule to determine the stage of development your puppy is currently experiencing. This knowledge will help you as you work with the puppy in the weeks and months ahead.

Period	Age	Characteristics
FIRST TO THIRD	BIRTH TO SEVEN WEEKS	Puppy needs food, sleep and warmth, and responds to simple and gentle touching. Needs mother for security and disciplining. Needs littermates for learning and interacting with other dogs. Pup learns to function within a pack and learns pack order of dominance. Begin socializing with adults and children for short periods. Begins to become aware of its environment.
FOURTH	EIGHT TO TWELVE WEEKS	Brain is fully developed. Needs socializing with outside world. Remove from mother and littermates. Needs to change from canine pack to human pack. Human dominance necessary. Fear period occurs between 8 and 16 weeks. Avoid fright and pain.
FIFTH	THIRTEEN TO SIXTEEN WEEKS	Training and formal obedience should begin. Less association with other dogs, more with people, places, situations. Period will pass easily if you remember this is pup's change-to-adolescence time. Be firm and fair. Flight instinct prominent. Permissiveness and over-disciplining can do permanent damage. Praise for good behavior.
JUVENILE	FOUR TO EIGHT MONTHS	Another fear period about 7 to 8 months of age. It passes quickly, but be cautious of fright and pain. Sexual maturity reached. Dominant traits established. Dog should understand sit, down, come and stay by now.

NOTE: THESE ARE APPROXIMATE TIME FRAMES. ALLOW FOR INDIVIDUAL DIFFERENCES IN PUPPIES.

house. If he goes during that time, praise him lavishly and take him indoors immediately. If he does not, but he has an accident when you go back indoors, pick him up immediately, say "No! No!" and return to his relief area. Wait a few minutes, then return to the house again. *Never* hit a puppy or put his face in urine or excrement when he has an accident! Such negativity solves nothing.

Once indoors, put the puppy in his crate until you have had time to clean up his accident. Then release him to the family area and watch him more closely than before. Chances are, his accident was a result of your not pick-

The most common surface on which to train a spaniel puppy is grass. This, of course, is the dog's natural terrain for relief and is the easiest and most accessible for most owners.

TAKE THE LEAD

Do not carry your dog to his relief area. Lead him there on a leash or, better yet, encourage him to follow you to the spot. If you start carrying him to his spot, you might end up doing this routine forever and your dog will have the satisfaction of having trained *you.*

ing up his signal or waiting too long before offering him the opportunity to relieve himself. Never hold a grudge against the puppy for accidents. He will sense your resentment.

Let the puppy learn that going outdoors means it is time to relieve himself, not play. Once trained, he will be able to play indoors and out and still differentiate between the times for play versus the times for relief.

Help him develop regular hours for naps, being alone, playing by himself and just resting, all in his crate. Encourage him to entertain himself while you are busy with your activities. Let him learn that having you near is comforting, but it is not your main purpose in life to provide him with undivided attention. Each time you put a puppy in his own area, use the same command, whatever suits best. Soon, he will run to his crate or special area when he hears you say those words.

Crate training provides safety for you, the puppy and the home. It also provides the puppy with a feeling of security, and that helps the puppy achieve self-confidence and clean habits. Remember that one of the primary ingredients in house-training your puppy is control. Regardless of your lifestyle, there will always be occasions when you will need to have a place where your dog can stay and be happy and safe. Crate training is the answer for now and in the future.

In conclusion, a few key elements are really all you need for a successful house-training method—consistency, frequency, praise, control and supervision. By following these procedures with a normal, healthy puppy, you and the puppy will soon be past the stage of accidents and

Once your Springer is used to his crate in the home, it will be easier to crate him for travel or other times when necessary.

ready to move on to a clean and rewarding life together.

ROLES OF DISCIPLINE, REWARD AND PUNISHMENT

Discipline, training one to act in accordance with rules, brings order to life. It is as simple as that. Without discipline, particularly in a group society, chaos reigns supreme and the group will eventually perish. Humans and canines are social animals and need some form of discipline in order to function effectively. They must procure food, reproduce to keep the species going and protect their home base and their young.

If there were no discipline in the lives of social animals, they would eventually die from starvation and/or predation by other stronger animals. In the case of domestic canines, dogs need discipline in their lives in order to

THE CLEAN LIFE

By providing sleeping and resting quarters that fit the dog, and offering frequent opportunities to relieve himself outside his quarters, the puppy quickly learns that the outdoors (or the newspaper if you are training him to paper) is the place to go when he needs to urinate or defecate. It also reinforces his innate desire to keep his sleeping quarters clean. This, in turn, helps develop the muscle control that will eventually produce a dog with clean living habits.

93

A wire crate offers many advantages for use in the home. Springers like to be a part of the action, and wire crates offer dogs a complete view of what's going on around them.

understand how their pack (you and other family members) functions and how they must act in order to survive.

A large humane society in a highly populated area recently surveyed dog owners regarding their satisfaction with their relationships with their dogs. People who had trained their dogs were 75% more satisfied with their pets than those who had never trained their dogs.

Dr. Edward Thorndike, a well-known psychologist, established *Thorndike's Theory of Learning*, which states that a behavior that results in a pleasant event tends to be repeated. Likewise, a behavior that results in an unpleasant event tends not to be repeated. It is this theory on which training methods are based today. For example, if you manipulate a dog to perform a specific behavior and reward him for doing it, he is likely to do it again because he enjoyed the end result.

Occasionally, punishment, a penalty inflicted for an offense, is necessary. The best type of punishment often comes from an

Be an ideal dog owner: clean up after your dog, whether it's in your own yard or a public place.

outside source. For example, a child is told not to touch the stove because he may get burned. He disobeys and touches the stove. In doing so, he receives a burn. From that time on, he respects the heat of the stove and avoids contact with it. Therefore, a behavior that results in an unpleasant event tends not to be repeated.

A good example of a dog learning the hard way is the dog who chases the house cat. He is told many times to leave the cat alone, yet he persists in teasing the cat. Then, one day he begins chasing the cat but the cat turns and swipes its claws across the dog's face, leaving him with a painful gash on his nose. The final result is that the dog stops chasing the cat.

TRAINING EQUIPMENT
COLLAR AND LEAD
For an English Springer Spaniel, the collar and lead that you use for training must be one with which you are easily able to work, not too heavy for the dog and

perfectly safe. Most owners opt for the lightweight nylon type, which are durable and affordable.

TREATS

Have a bag of treats on hand. Something nutritious and easy to swallow works best. Use a soft treat, a chunk of cheese or a piece of cooked chicken rather than a dry biscuit. By the time the dog gets done chewing a dry treat, he will forget why he is being rewarded in the first place! Using food rewards will not teach a dog to beg at the table—the only way to teach a dog to beg at the table is to give him food from the table. In training, rewarding the dog with a food treat will help him associate praise and the treats with learning new behaviors that obviously please his owner.

TRAINING BEGINS:
ASK THE DOG A QUESTION

In order to teach your dog anything, you must first get his attention. After all, he cannot learn anything if he is looking away from you with his mind on something else.

To get his attention, ask him "School?" and immediately walk over to him and give him a treat as you tell him "Good dog." Wait a minute or two and repeat the routine, this time with a treat in your hand as you approach within a foot of the dog. Do not go directly to him, but stop about a

Your Springer will learn the rewards of proper behavior when food treats, along with your praise, are used as motivators in training.

foot short of him and hold out the treat as you ask, "School?" He will see you approaching with a treat in your hand and most likely begin walking toward you. As you meet, give him the treat and praise again.

The third time, ask the question, have a treat in your hand and walk only a short distance

FAMILY TIES

If you have other pets in the home and/or interact often with the pets of friends and other family members, your pup will respond to those pets in much the same manner as you do. It is only when you show fear of or resentment toward another animal that he will act fearful or unfriendly.

Getting and keeping your Springer's attention are necessary before teaching something new.

toward the dog so that he must walk almost all the way to you. As he reaches you, give him the treat and praise again.

By this time, the dog will probably be getting the idea that if he pays attention to you, espe-

COMMAND STANCE
Stand up straight and authoritatively when giving your dog commands. Do not issue commands when lying on the floor or lying on your back on the sofa. If you are on your hands and knees when you give a command, your dog will think you are positioning yourself to play.

cially when you ask that question, it will pay off in treats and fun activities for him. In other words, he learns that "school" means doing fun things with you that result in treats and positive attention for him.

Remember that the dog does not understand your verbal language, he only recognizes sounds. Your question translates to a series of sounds for him, and those sounds become the signal to go to you and pay attention; if he does, he will get to interact with you plus receive treats and praise.

THE BASIC COMMANDS
TEACHING SIT
Now that you have the dog's attention, attach his lead and hold it in your left hand and a food treat in your right. Place your food hand at the dog's nose and let him lick the treat but do not let him take it from you. Say "Sit" and slowly raise your food hand from in front of the dog's nose up over his head so that he is looking at the ceiling. As he bends his head upward, he will have to bend his knees to maintain his balance. As he bends his knees, he will assume a sit position. At that point, release the food treat and praise lavishly with comments such as "Good dog! Good sit!" Remember to always praise enthusiastically, because dogs relish verbal praise from their owners and feel so proud of themselves

whenever they accomplish a good behavior.

You will not use food forever in getting the dog to obey your commands. Food is only used to teach new behaviors, and once the dog knows what you want when you give a specific command, you will wean him off the food treats but still offer the verbal praise. After all, you will always have your voice with you, and there will be many times when you have no food rewards but expect the dog to obey.

TEACHING DOWN

Teaching the down exercise is easy when you understand how the dog perceives the down position, but it is very difficult when you do not. Dogs perceive the down position as a submissive one, therefore teaching the down exercise using a forceful method can sometimes make the dog develop such a fear of the down that he either runs away when you say "Down" or he attempts to snap at the person who tries to force him down.

DOUBLE JEOPARDY

A dog in jeopardy never lies down. He stays alert on his feet because instinct tells him that he may have to run away or fight for his survival. Therefore, if a dog feels threatened or anxious, he will not lie down. Consequently, it is important to keep the dog calm and relaxed as he learns the down exercise.

Have the dog sit close along-side your left leg, facing in the same direction as you are. Hold the lead in your left hand and a food treat in your right. Now place your left hand lightly on the top of the dog's shoulders where they meet above the spinal cord. Do not push down on the dog's shoulders; simply rest your left hand there so you can guide the dog to lie down close to your left leg rather than to swing away from your side when he drops.

Now place the food hand at the dog's nose, say "Down" very

Practice the down command in a non-threatening, familiar environment. Your Springer's commands must be reinforced regularly to keep them sharp.

97

softly (almost a whisper), and slowly lower the food hand to the dog's front feet. When the food hand reaches the floor, begin moving it forward along the floor in front of the dog. Keep talking softly to the dog, saying things like, "Do you want this treat? You can do this, good dog." Your reassuring tone of voice will help calm the dog as he tries to follow the food hand in order to get the treat.

When the dog's elbows touch the floor, release the food and praise softly. Try to get the dog to maintain that down position for several seconds before you let him sit up again. The goal here is to get the dog to settle down and not feel threatened in the down position.

TEACHING STAY

It is easy to teach the dog to stay in either a sit or a down position. Again, we use food and praise during the teaching process as we help the dog to understand exactly what it is that we are expecting him to do.

To teach the sit/stay, start with the dog sitting on your left side as before and hold the lead in your left hand. Have a food treat in your right hand and place your food hand at the dog's nose. Say "Stay" and step out on your right foot to stand directly in front of the dog, toe to toe, as he licks and nibbles the treat. Be sure to keep his head facing upward to maintain the sit position. Count to five and then swing around to stand next to the dog again with him on your left. As soon as you get back to the original position, release the food and praise lavishly.

To teach the down/stay, do the down as previously described. As soon as the dog lies down, say "Stay" and step out on your right foot just as you did in the sit/stay. Count to five and then return to stand beside the dog with him on your left side. Release the treat and praise as always.

Within a week or ten days, you can begin to add a bit of distance between you and your dog when you leave him. When you do, use your left hand open with the palm facing the dog as a

LANGUAGE BARRIER

Dogs do not understand our language and have to rely on tone of voice more than just works or sound. They can be trained to react to a certain sound, at a certain volume. If you say "No, Oliver" in a very soft, pleasant voice, it will not have the same meaning as "No, Oliver!!" when you shout it as loud as you can. You should never use the dog's name during a reprimand, just the command "No! "

You never want the dog to associate his name with a negative experience or reprimand.

This Springer demonstrates his ability to perform the down/stay command in an agility trial.

stay signal, much the same as the hand signal a police officer uses to stop traffic at an intersection. Hold the food treat in your right hand as before, but this time the food is not touching the dog's nose. He will watch the food hand and quickly learn that he is going to get that treat as soon as you return to his side.

When you can stand 1 yard away from your dog for 30 seconds, you can then begin building time and distance in both stays. Eventually, the dog can be expected to remain in the stay position for prolonged periods of time until you return to him or call him to you. Always praise lavishly when he stays.

TEACHING COME

If you make teaching "come" a fun experience, you should never have a student that does not love the game or that fails to come when called. The secret, it seems, is never to teach the word "come."

At times when an owner most wants his dog to come when called, the owner is likely upset or anxious and he allows these feelings to come through in the tone of his voice when he calls his dog. Hearing that desperation in his owner's voice, the dog fears the results of going to him and therefore either disobeys outright or runs in the opposite direction. The secret, therefore, is to teach

99

the dog a game and, when you want him to come to you, simply play the game. It is practically a no-fail solution!

To begin, have several members of your family take a few food treats and each go into a different room in the house. Take turns calling the dog, and each person should celebrate the dog's finding him with a treat and lots of happy praise. When a person calls the dog, he is actually inviting the dog to find him and get a treat as a reward for "winning."

A few turns of the "Where are you?" game and the dog will figure out that everyone is playing the game and that each person has a big celebration awaiting his

success at locating them. Once he learns to love the game, simply calling out "Where are you?" will bring him running from wherever he is when he hears that all-important question.

The come command is recognized as one of the most important things to teach a dog, but there are trainers who work with thousands of dogs and never teach the actual word "come." Yet these dogs will race to respond to a person who uses the dog's name followed by "Where are you?" For example, a woman has a 12-year-old companion dog who went blind, but who never fails to locate her owner when asked, "Where are you?"

Children particularly love to play this game with their dogs. Children can hide in smaller places like a shower or bathtub, behind a bed or under a table. The dog needs to work a little bit harder to find these hiding places, but when he does he loves to celebrate with a treat and a tussle with a favorite youngster.

TEACHING HEEL

Heeling means that the dog walks beside the owner without pulling. It takes time and patience on the owner's part to succeed at teaching the dog that he (the owner) will not proceed unless the dog is walking calmly beside him. Pulling out ahead on the lead is definitely not acceptable.

PRACTICE MAKES PERFECT!

• Have training lessons with your dog every day in several short segments—three to five times a day for a few minutes at a time is ideal.

• Do not have long practice sessions. The dog will become easily bored.

• Never practice when you are tired, ill, worried or in an otherwise negative mood. This will transmit to the dog and may have an adverse effect on his performance.

Think fun, short and above all *positive*! End each session on a high note, rather than a failed exercise, and make sure to give a lot of praise. Enjoy the training and help your dog enjoy it, too.

Begin with holding the lead in your left hand as the dog sits beside your left leg. Move the loop end of the lead to your right hand but keep your left hand short on the lead so it keeps the dog in close next to you.

Say "Heel" and step forward on your left foot. Keep the dog close to you and take three steps. Stop and have the dog sit next to you in what we now call the heel position. Praise verbally, but do not touch the dog. Hesitate a moment and begin again with "Heel," taking three steps and stopping, at which point the dog is told to sit again.

Your goal here is to have the dog walk those three steps without pulling on the lead. When he will walk calmly beside you for three steps without pulling, increase the

"COME" . . . BACK

Never call your dog to come to you for a correction or scold him when he reaches you. That is the quickest way to turn a come command into "Go away fast!" Dogs think only in the present tense, and your dog will connect the scolding with coming to you, not with the misbehavior of a few moments earlier.

101

number of steps you take to five. When he will walk politely beside you while you take five steps, you can increase the length of your walk to ten steps. Keep increasing the length of your stroll until the dog will walk quietly beside you without pulling as long as you want him to heel. When you stop heeling, indicate to the dog that the exercise is over by verbally praising as you pet him and say "OK, good dog." The "OK" is used as a release word, meaning that the exercise is finished and the dog is free to relax.

If you are dealing with a dog who insists on pulling you around, simply "put on your brakes" and stand your ground until the dog realizes that the two of you are not going anywhere until he is beside you and moving at your pace, not his. It may take some time just standing there to convince the dog that you are the leader and you will be the one to decide on the direction and speed of your travel.

Each time the dog looks up at you or slows down to give a slack lead between the two of you, quietly praise him and say, "Good heel. Good dog." Eventually, the dog will begin to respond and within a few days he will be walking politely beside you without pulling on the lead. At first, the training sessions should be kept short and very positive; soon the dog will be able to walk nicely with you for increasingly longer distances. Remember also to give the dog free time and the opportunity to run and play when you are done with heel practice.

WEANING OFF FOOD IN TRAINING

Food is used in training new behaviors. Once the dog understands what behavior goes with a specific command, it is time to start weaning him off the food treats. At first, give a treat after each exercise. Then, start to give a treat only after every other

TUG OF WALK?

If you begin teaching the heel by taking long walks and letting the dog pull you along, he misinterprets this action as an acceptable form of taking a walk. When you pull back on the lead to counteract his pulling, he reads that tug as a signal to pull even harder!

exercise. Mix up the times when you offer a food reward and the times when you only offer praise so that the dog will never know when he is going to receive both food and praise and when he is going to receive only praise. This is called a variable ratio reward system and it proves successful because there is always the chance that the owner will produce a treat, so the dog never stops trying for that reward. No matter what, always give verbal praise.

OBEDIENCE CLASSES
It is a good idea to enroll in an obedience class if one is available in your area. If yours is a show dog, handling classes would be more appropriate. Many areas have dog clubs that offer basic obedience training as well as preparatory classes for obedience competition. There are also local dog trainers who offer similar classes.

At obedience trials, dogs can earn titles at various levels of competition. The beginning levels of competition include basic behaviors such as sit, down, heel, etc. The more advanced levels of competition include jumping, retrieving, scent discrimination and signal work. The advanced levels require a dog and owner to put a lot of time and effort into their training and the titles that can be earned

at these levels of competition are very prestigious.

OTHER ACTIVITIES FOR LIFE
Whether a dog is trained in the structured environment of a class or alone with his owner at home, there are many activities that can

Once your Springer is house-trained and proficient in basic commands, the everyday routine will become second nature to him. These Springers wait politely by the door to be let back inside.

REAP THE REWARDS
If you start with a normal, healthy dog and give him time, patience and some carefully executed lessons, you will reap the rewards of that training for the life of the dog. And what a life it will be! The two of you will find immeasurable pleasure in the companionship you have built together with love, respect and understanding.

103

A well-trained hunting spaniel works competently in water as well as the field. This Springer is retrieving a bumper (dummy) from the water as a part of a training exercise.

bring fun and rewards to both owner and dog once they have mastered basic control.

Teaching the dog to help out around the home, in the yard or on the farm provides great satisfaction to both dog and owner. In addition, the dog's help makes life a little easier for his owner and raises his stature as a valued companion to his family. It helps give the dog a purpose by occupying his mind and providing an outlet for his energy.

Springers can be trained to participate in many fun activities...although this Springer seems to have found something more interesting than his "sled-dog" duties.

KEEP SMILING

Never train your dog, puppy or adult, when you are angry or in a sour mood. Dogs are very sensitive to human feelings, especially anger, and if your dog senses that you are angry or upset, he will connect your anger with his training and learn to resent or fear his training sessions.

OBEDIENCE SCHOOL

Taking your dog to an obedience school may be the best investment in time and money you can ever make. You will enjoy the benefits for the lifetime of your dog and you will have the opportunity to meet people who have similar expectations for companion dogs.

Backpacking is an exciting and healthy activity that the dog can be taught without assistance from more than his owner. The exercise of walking and climbing is good for man and dog alike, and the bond that they develop together is priceless.

If you are interested in participating in organized competition with your English Springer Spaniel, there are activities other than obedience in which you and your dog can become involved. Agility is a popular and fun sport where dogs run through an obstacle course that includes various jumps, tunnels and other exercises to test the dog's speed and coordination. The owners run through the course beside their dogs to give commands and to guide them through the course. Although competitive, the focus is on fun—it's fun to do, fun to watch, and great exercise.

FIELD TRAINING

The spaniel's duties in the field consist of working close to the sportsman, to quest for game, flush it and retrieve it when called upon to do so. The Springer is the dog for the rough shooter, i.e., the man who goes out by himself in search of game, be it fur or feather.

If you want to train your Springer Spaniel for work, you have to start at an early age. The basis for every training is obedience and that is where you start

Training your Springer to hand signals is an advanced form of training. Start using hand signals along with verbal commands to teach your dog their meaning.

a trail for him to work out. You can also throw the dummy into light cover, out of sight, and encourage your Springer to locate and then retrieve it. You must be very careful with the puppy when he starts teething because picking up the dummy might be quite painful and forcing him to pick it up would do irreparable harm to his willingness to retrieve. By the time your puppy is eight or nine months old, knows his basic obedience and has learned to retrieve and use his nose, you can join a training class. Depending on his natural aptitude, you can train for many different pursuits, from working and spaniel tests to tracking and more.

Springers often do well in agility trials. This Springer conquers the obstacles with ease.

The English Springer Spaniel is a sporting dog by instinct and will respond to being trained for work at an early age.

with your puppy immediately. Everything he learns when he is under six months old won't be forgotten. You can also start to teach him to retrieve a small object or dummy. This can be a sock or a rabbit skin or a wing of a bird. If you throw the object a few yards ahead of your puppy, he will run to it and pick it up. Call him by his name and encourage him to bring it back to you. Don't be discouraged if your puppy thinks this is a fun game and runs off with the object! If he does that, move away from him, calling him by his name. Always remember to reward him whenever possible.

The next lesson is to encourage him to use his nose. By dragging a piece of meat you can make

Springers are trained to retrieve dummies before they are used to retrieve game. Springers are known to have "soft mouths," meaning that they exert minimum pressure on whatever they carry in their mouths so as not to damage it.

A BORN PRODIGY

Occasionally, a dog and owner who have not attended formal classes have been able to earn entry-level titles by obtaining competition rules and regulations from a local kennel club and practicing on their own to a degree of perfection. Obtaining the higher level titles, however, almost always requires extensive training under the tutelage of experienced instructors. In addition, the more difficult levels require more specialized equipment whereas the lower levels do not.

Retrieving over a fence—a working Springer's job is to bring the game (or, in this case, the dummy) to his master, without letting anything get in his way.

107

Above: Candid photos of an actual hunt. The English Springer Spaniels are alert and ready to work.

Opposite page:
(Top) The Springer successfully returns the dummy to his master.
(Bottom) Using hand signals, the owner commands the dog to "Down/stay."

109

Internal Organs with Skeletal Structure

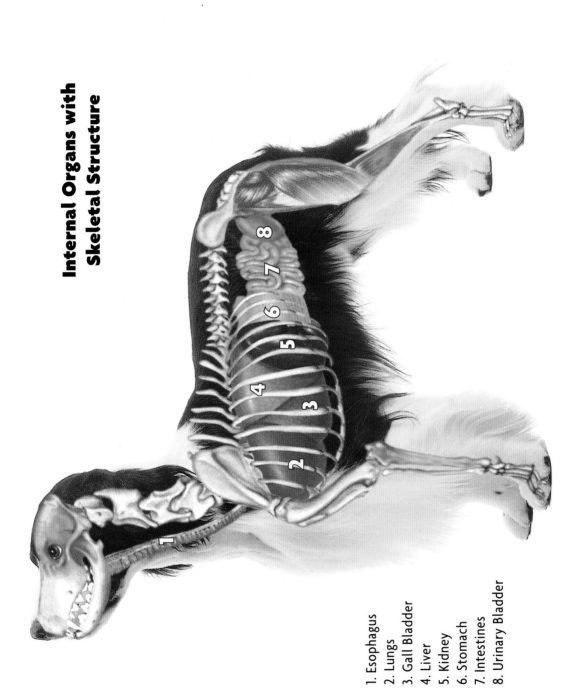

1. Esophagus
2. Lungs
3. Gall Bladder
4. Liver
5. Kidney
6. Stomach
7. Intestines
8. Urinary Bladder

Health Care of Your
ENGLISH SPRINGER SPANIEL

Dogs suffer from many of the same physical illnesses as people. Since most people know more about human diseases than canine maladies, many of the terms used in this chapter will be familiar but not necessarily those used by veterinarians. We will use the term *x-ray*, instead of the more acceptable term *radiograph*. We will also use the familiar term *symptoms* even though dogs don't have symptoms, which are verbal descriptions of the patient's feelings—dogs have *clinical signs*. Since dogs can't speak, we have to look for clinical signs...but we still use the term *symptoms* in this book.

As a general rule, medicine is *practiced*. That term is not arbitrary. Medicine is a constantly changing art as we learn more and more about genetics, electronic aids (like CAT scans and MRIs) and daily laboratory advances. There are many dog maladies, like canine hip dysplasia, which are not universally treated in the same manner. Some veterinarians opt for surgery more often than others do.

SELECTING A VETERINARIAN

Your selection of a veterinarian should be based not only upon personality and ability with sporting dogs but also upon his convenience to your home. You want a vet who is close because you might have emergencies or need to make multiple visits for treatments. You want a vet who has

Before you buy your English Springer Spaniel, meet and interview the veterinarians in your area. Take everything into consideration—discuss his background, specialties, fees, emergency policy, etc.

Breakdown of Veterinary Income by Category

2%	Dentistry
4%	Radiology
12%	Surgery
15%	Vaccinations
19%	Laboratory
23%	Examinations
25%	Medicines

A typical vet's income categorized according to services performed. This survey dealt with small-animal (pet) practices.

services that you might require such as grooming facilities as well as sophisticated pet supplies and a good reputation for ability and responsiveness. There is nothing more frustrating than having to wait a day or more to get a response from your veterinarian.

All veterinarians are licensed and their diplomas and/or certificates should be displayed in their waiting rooms. There are, however, many veterinary specialties that usually require further studies and internships. There are specialists in heart problems (veterinary cardiologists), skin problems (veterinary dermatologists), teeth and gum problems (veterinary dentists), eye problems (veterinary ophthalmologists), x-rays (veterinary radiologists), and surgeons who have specialties in bones,

muscles or other organs. Most veterinarians do routine surgery such as neutering, stitching up wounds and docking tails for those breeds in which such is required for show purposes. When the problem affecting your dog is serious, it is not unusual or impudent to get another medical opinion, although it is courteous to advise the vets concerned about this. You might also want to compare costs among several veterinarians. Sophisticated health care and veterinary services can be very costly. Don't be bashful about discussing these costs with your veterinarian or his staff. It is not infrequent that important decisions are based upon financial considerations.

PREVENTATIVE MEDICINE
It is much easier, less costly and more effective to practice preventative medicine than to fight bouts of illness and disease. Properly bred puppies come from parents that were selected based upon their genetic-disease profiles. Their dam should have been vaccinated, free of all internal and external parasites, and properly nourished. For these reasons, a visit to the veterinarian who cared for the dam is recommended. The dam can pass on disease resistance to her puppies, which can last for eight to ten weeks. She can also pass

First Aid
at a Glance

Burns
Place the affected area under cool water; use ice if only a small area is burnt.

Bee stings
Apply ice to relieve swelling; antihistamine dosed properly.

Animal bites
Clean any bleeding area; apply pressure until bleeding subsides; go to the vet.

Spider bites
Use cold compress and a pressurized pack to inhibit venom's spreading.

Antifreeze poisoning
Immediately induce vomiting by using hydrogen peroxide.

Fish hooks
Removal best handled by vet; hook must be cut in order to remove.

Snake bites
Pack ice around bite; contact vet quickly; identify snake for proper antivenin.

Car accident
Move dog from roadway with blanket; seek veterinary aid.

Shock
Calm the dog, keep him warm; seek immediate veterinary help.

Nosebleed
Apply cold compress to the nose; apply pressure to any visible abrasion.

Bleeding
Apply pressure above the area; treat wound by applying a cotton pack.

Heat stroke
Submerge dog in cold bath; cool down with fresh air and water; go to the vet.

Frostbite/Hypothermia
Warm the dog with a warm bath, electric blankets or hot water bottles.

Abrasions
Clean the wound and wash out thoroughly with fresh water; apply antiseptic.

Remember: an injured dog may attempt to bite a helping hand from fear and confusion. Always muzzle the dog before trying to offer assistance.

HEALTH AND VACCINATION SCHEDULE

Age in Weeks:	3rd	6th	8th	10th	12th	14th	16th	20-24th
Worm Control	✔	✔	✔	✔	✔	✔	✔	✔
Neutering								✔
Heartworm		✔						✔
Parvovirus		✔		✔		✔		✔
Distemper			✔		✔		✔	
Hepatitis			✔		✔		✔	
Leptospirosis		✔		✔		✔		
Parainfluenza		✔		✔		✔		
Dental Examination			✔					✔
Complete Physical			✔					✔
Temperament Testing			✔					
Coronavirus					✔			
Canine Cough		✔						
Hip Dysplasia							✔	
Rabies								✔

Vaccinations are not instantly effective. It takes about two weeks for the dog's immune system to develop antibodies. Most vaccinations require annual booster shots. Your veterinarian should guide you in this regard.

An English Springer Spaniel getting a routine examination.

VACCINE ALLERGIES

Vaccines do not work all the time. Sometimes dogs are allergic to them and many times the antibodies, which are supposed to be stimulated by the vaccine, just are not produced. You should keep your dog in the veterinary clinic for an hour after it is vaccinated to be sure there are no allergic reactions.

on parasites and many infections. That's why you should visit the veterinarian who cared for the dam.

WEANING TO FIVE MONTHS OLD
Puppies should be weaned by the time they are about two months old. A puppy that remains for at least eight weeks with his dam and littermates usually adapts better to other dogs and people later in life.

Some new owners have their puppy examined by a veterinarian immediately, that is a good idea. Vaccination programs usually begin when the puppy is very young.

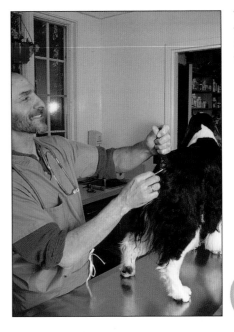

The veterinarian takes the Springer's temperature.

Disease	What is it?	What causes it?	Symptoms
Leptospirosis	Severe disease that affects the internal organs; can be spread to people.	A bacterium, which is often carried by rodents, that enters through mucous membranes and spreads quickly throughout the body.	Range from fever, vomiting and loss of appetite in less severe cases to shock, irreversible kidney damage and possibly death in most severe cases.
Rabies	Potentially deadly virus that infects warm-blooded mammals.	Bite from a carrier of the virus, mainly wild animals.	1st stage: dog exhibits change in behavior, fear. 2nd stage: dog's behavior becomes more aggressive. 3rd stage: loss of coordination, trouble with bodily functions.
Parvovirus	Highly contagious virus, potentially deadly.	Ingestion of the virus, which is usually spread through the feces of infected dogs.	Most common: severe diarrhea. Also vomiting, fatigue, lack of appetite.
Canine cough	Contagious respiratory infection.	Combination of types of bacteria and virus. Most common: *Bordetella bronchiseptica* bacteria and parainfluenza virus.	Chronic cough.
Distemper	Disease primarily affecting respiratory and nervous system.	Virus that is related to the human measles virus.	Mild symptoms such as fever, lack of appetite and mucus secretion progress to evidence of brain damage, "hard pad."
Hepatitis	Virus primarily affecting the liver.	Canine adenovirus type I (CAV-1). Enters system when dog breathes in particles.	Lesser symptoms include listlessness, diarrhea, vomiting. More severe symptoms include "blue-eye" (clumps of virus in eye).
Coronavirus	Virus resulting in digestive problems.	Virus is spread through infected dog's feces.	Stomach upset evidenced by lack of appetite, vomiting, diarrhea.

A litter of healthy Springer puppies will have been inoculated and wormed before going to new homes. Discuss the booster-shot program with your breeder before bringing your puppy home.

A litter of healthy Springer puppies will have been inoculated and wormed before going to new homes. Discuss the booster-shot program with your breeder before bringing your puppy home.

The puppy will have his teeth examined and have his skeletal conformation and general health checked prior to certification by the veterinarian. Puppies in certain breeds have problems with their kneecaps, cataracts and other eye problems, heart murmurs and undescended testicles. They may also have personality problems and your veterinarian might have training in temperament evaluation.

Vaccination Scheduling

Most vaccinations are given by injection and should only be done by a veterinarian. Both he and you should keep a record of the date of the injection, the identification of the vaccine and the amount given. Some vets give a first vaccination at eight weeks, but most dog breeders prefer the course not to commence until about ten weeks because of negating any antibodies passed on by the dam. The vaccination scheduling is usually based on a 15-day cycle. You must take your vet's advice as to when to vaccinate as this may differ according to the vaccine used. Most vaccinations immunize your puppy against viruses.

The usual vaccines contain immunizing doses of several different viruses such as distemper, parvovirus, parainfluenza and hepatitis. There are other vaccines available when the puppy is at risk. You should rely upon professional advice. This is especially true for the booster-shot program. Most vaccination programs require a booster when the puppy is a year old and once a year thereafter. In some cases, circumstances may require more or less frequent immunizations.

Canine cough, more formally known as tracheobronchitis, is treated with a vaccine that is sprayed into the dog's nostrils.

CUSHING'S DISEASE

Cases of hyperactive adrenal glands (Cushing's disease) have been traced to the drinking of highly chlorinated water. Aerate or age your dog's drinking water before offering it.

Normal English Springer Spaniel Skeleton

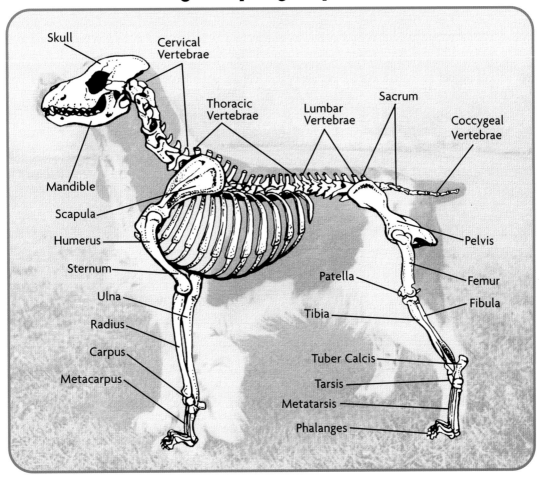

Skull
Cervical Vertebrae
Thoracic Vertebrae
Lumbar Vertebrae
Sacrum
Coccygeal Vertebrae
Mandible
Scapula
Humerus
Sternum
Ulna
Radius
Carpus
Metacarpus
Pelvis
Femur
Patella
Fibula
Tibia
Tuber Calcis
Tarsis
Metatarsis
Phalanges

Canine cough is usually included in routine vaccination, but this is often not so effective as for other major diseases.

FIVE MONTHS TO ONE YEAR OF AGE
Unless you intend to breed or show your dog, neutering the puppy at six months of age is recommended. Discuss this with your veterinarian. Neutering and spaying have proven to be extremely beneficial to both male and female dogs. Besides eliminating the possibility of pregnancy, it inhibits (but does not prevent) breast cancer in bitches and prostate cancer in male dogs. Under no circumstances should a bitch be spayed prior to her first season.

OVER ONE YEAR OF AGE
Continue to visit the veterinarian at least once a year. There is no such disease as old age, but bodily

DENTAL HEALTH

A dental examination is in order when the dog is between six months and one year of age so that any permanent teeth that have erupted incorrectly can be corrected. It is important to begin a brushing routine and remain consistent with it throughout the dog's lifetime. Durable nylon and safe edible chews should be a part of your puppy's arsenal for good health, good teeth and pleasant breath. The vast majority of dogs three to four years old and older has diseases of the gums from lack of dental attention. Using the various types of dental chews can be very effective in controlling dental plaque.

functions do change with age. The eyes and ears are no longer as efficient. Liver, kidney and intestinal functions often decline. Proper dietary changes, recommended by your veterinarian, can make life more pleasant for the aging English Springer Spaniel and you.

SKIN PROBLEMS IN ENGLISH SPRINGER SPANIELS

Veterinarians are consulted by dog owners for skin problems more than any other group of diseases or maladies. Dogs' skin is almost as sensitive as human skin and both suffer almost the same ailments (though the occurrence of acne in dogs is rare). For this reason, veterinary dermatology has developed into a specialty practiced by many veterinarians.

Since many skin problems have visual symptoms that are almost identical, it requires the skill of an experienced veterinary dermatologist to identify and cure many of the more severe skin disorders. Pet shops sell many treatments for skin problems but most of the treatments are directed at symptoms and not the underlying problem(s). If your dog is suffering from a skin disorder, you should seek professional assistance as quickly as possible. As with all diseases, the earlier a problem is identified and treated, the more successful is the cure.

HEREDITARY SKIN DISORDERS

Veterinary dermatologists are currently researching a number of skin disorders that are believed to have a hereditary basis. These inherited diseases are transmitted by both parents, who appear (phenotypically) normal but have a recessive gene for the disease, meaning that they carry, but are not affected by, the disease. These diseases pose serious problems to breeders because in some instances there are no methods of identifying carriers. Often the secondary diseases associated with these skin conditions are even more debilitating than the skin disorders themselves, including cancers and respiratory problems.

Among the hereditary skin disorders, for which the mode of inheritance is known, are acrodermatitis, cutaneous asthenia (Ehlers-Danlos syndrome), sebaceous adenitis, cyclic hematopoiesis, dermatomyositis, IgA deficiency, color dilution alopecia and nodular dermatofibrosis. Some of these disorders are limited to one or two breeds, while others affect a large number of breeds. All inherited diseases must be diagnosed and treated by a veterinary specialist.

PROPER DIET

Feeding your dog properly is very important. An incorrect diet could affect the dog's health, behavior and nervous system, possibly making a normal dog into an aggressive one. Its most visible effects are to the skin and coat, but internal organs are similarly affected.

PARASITE BITES

Many of us are allergic to insect bites. The bites itch, erupt and may even become infected. Dogs have the same reaction to fleas, ticks and/or mites. When an insect lands on you, you have the chance to whisk it away with your hand. Unfortunately, when your dog is bitten by a flea, tick or mite, he can only scratch it away or bite it. By the time the dog has been bitten, the parasite has done some of its damage. It may also have laid eggs to cause further problems in the near future. The itching from parasite bites is probably due to the saliva injected into the site when the parasite sucks the dog's blood.

AUTO-IMMUNE SKIN CONDITIONS

Auto-immune skin conditions are commonly referred to as being allergic to yourself, while allergies are usually inflammatory reactions to an outside stimulus. Auto-immune diseases cause serious damage to the tissues that are involved.

The best known auto-immune disease is lupus, which affects people as well as dogs. The symptoms are variable and may affect the kidneys, bones, blood chemistry and skin. It can be fatal to both dogs and humans, though it is not thought to be transmissible. It is usually successfully treated with cortisone, prednisone or similar corticosteroid, but extensive use of these drugs can have harmful side effects.

AIRBORNE ALLERGIES

Just as humans have hay fever, rose fever and other fevers from which they suffer during the pollinating season, many dogs suffer from the same allergies. When the pollen count is high, your dog might suffer but don't expect him to sneeze and have a runny nose as a human would. Dogs react to pollen allergies the same way they react to fleas—they scratch and bite themselves.

Dogs, like humans, can be tested for allergens. Discuss the testing with your veterinary dermatologist.

FOOD PROBLEMS

FOOD ALLERGIES

Dogs are allergic to many foods that are best sellers and highly recommended by breeders and veterinarians. Changing the brand of food that you buy may not eliminate the problem if the element to which the dog is allergic is contained in the new brand.

Recognizing a food allergy is difficult. Humans vomit or have rashes when they eat a food to which they are allergic. Dogs neither vomit nor (usually) develop a rash. They react in the same manner as they do to an airborne or flea allergy: they itch, scratch and bite. Thus making the diagnosis extremely difficult. While pollen allergies and parasite bites are usually seasonal, food allergies are year-round problems.

FOOD INTOLERANCE

Food intolerance is the inability of the dog to completely digest certain foods. For example, puppies that may have done very well on their dam's milk may not do well on cow's milk. The result of this food intolerance may be loose bowels, pass-

Dogs, like humans, can be allergic to certain foods. For this reason, find a well-balanced dog food and do not change the brand. Additional supplements are not necessary unless recommended by the vet.

Check your Springer's stool from time to time. He should not be straining, and the stool should be well formed and with no indication of worms.

ing gas and stomach pains. These are the only obvious symptoms of food intolerance and that makes diagnosis difficult.

TREATING FOOD PROBLEMS

It is possible to handle food allergies and food intolerance yourself. Put your dog on a diet that he has never had. Obviously if he has never eaten this new food, he can't have been allergic or intolerant of it. Start with a single ingredient that is not in the dog's diet at the present time, such as raw tripe and wholemeal bread. Keep the dog on this diet (with no additives) for a month. If the symptoms of food allergy or intolerance

disappear, don't go back to his old diet, but stick to the tripe and bread and add one ingredient of his former diet. Let the dog stay on the modified diet for a month before you add another ingredient. It will take some time but you will find out which is the ingredient that caused the problems.

An alternative method is to carefully study the ingredients in the diet to which your dog is allergic or intolerant. Identify the main ingredient in this diet and eliminate the main ingredient by buying a different food that does not have that ingredient. Keep experimenting until the symptoms disappear after one month on the new diet.

121

A male dog flea, *Ctenocephalides canis.*

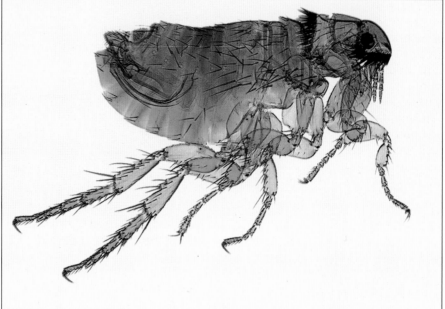

PHOTO BY JEAN CLAUDE REVY/PHOTOTAKE.

EXTERNAL PARASITES

FLEAS

Of all the problems to which dogs are prone, none is more well known and frustrating than fleas. Flea infestation is relatively simple to cure but difficult to prevent. Parasites that are harbored inside the body are a bit more difficult to eradicate but they are easier to control.

To control flea infestation, you have to understand the flea's life cycle. Fleas are often thought of as a summertime problem, but centrally heated homes have changed the patterns and fleas can be found at any time of the year. The most effective method of flea control is a two-stage approach: one stage to kill the adult fleas, and the other to control the development of pre-adult fleas. Unfortunately, no single active ingredient is effective against all stages of the life cycle.

FLEA KILLER CAUTION— "POISON"

Flea-killers are poisonous. You should not spray these toxic chemicals on areas of a dog's body that he licks, including his genitals and his face. Flea killers taken internally are a better answer, but check with your vet in case internal therapy is not advised for your dog.

LIFE CYCLE STAGES

During its life, a flea will pass through four life stages: egg, larva, pupa or nymph and adult. The adult stage is the most visible and irritating stage of the flea life cycle, and this is why the majority of flea-control products concentrate on this stage. The fact is that adult fleas account for only 1% of the total flea population, and the other 99% exist in pre-adult stages, i.e., eggs, larvae and nymphs. The pre-adult stages are barely visible to the naked eye.

THE LIFE CYCLE OF THE FLEA

Eggs are laid on the dog, usually in quantities of about 20 or 30, several times a day. The adult female flea must have a blood meal before each egg-laying session. When first laid, the eggs will cling to the dog's hair, as the eggs are still moist. However, they will quickly dry out and fall from the dog, especially if the dog moves around or scratches. Many eggs will fall off in the dog's favorite area or an area in which he spends a lot of time, such as his bed.

Once the eggs fall from the dog onto the carpet or furniture, they will hatch into larvae. This takes from one to ten days. Larvae are not particularly mobile and will usually travel only a few inches from where they hatch. However, they do have a tendency to move away from bright light and heavy

EN GARDE:
CATCHING FLEAS OFF GUARD!
Consider the following ways to arm yourself against fleas:
- Add a small amount of pennyroyal or eucalyptus oil to your dog's bath. These natural remedies repel fleas.
- Supplement your dog's food with fresh garlic (minced or grated) and an hearty amount of brewer's yeast, both of which ward off fleas.
- Use a flea comb on your dog daily. Submerge fleas in a cup of bleach to kill them quickly.
- Confine the dog to only a few rooms to limit the spread of fleas in the home.
- Vacuum daily...and get all of the crevices! Dispose of the bag every few days until the problem is under control.
- Wash your dog's bedding daily. Cover cushions where your dog sleeps with towels, and wash the towels often.

traffic—under furniture and behind doors are common places to find high quantities of flea larvae.

The flea larvae feed on dead organic matter, including adult flea feces, until they are ready to change into adult fleas. Fleas will usually remain as larvae for around seven days. After this period, the larvae will pupate into protective pupae. While inside the pupae, the larvae will undergo metamorphosis and change into adult fleas. This can take as little time as a few days, but the adult fleas can remain inside the pupae waiting to hatch for up to two years. The pupae are signaled to hatch by certain stimuli, such as physical pressure—the pupae's being stepped on, heat from an animal's lying on the pupae or increased carbon-dioxide levels and vibrations—indicating that a suitable host is available.

Once hatched, the adult flea must feed within a few days. Once the adult flea finds a host, it will not leave voluntarily. It only becomes dislodged by grooming or the host animal's scratching.

The adult flea will remain on the host for the duration of its life unless forcibly removed.

TREATING THE ENVIRONMENT AND THE DOG

Treating fleas should be a two-pronged attack. First, the environment needs to be treated; this includes carpets and furniture, especially the dog's bedding and areas underneath furniture. The environment should be treated with a household spray containing an Insect Growth Regulator (IGR) and an insecticide to kill the adult fleas. Most IGRs are effective against eggs and larvae; they actually mimic the fleas' own hormones and stop the eggs and larvae from developing into adult fleas. There are currently no treatments available to attack the pupa stage of the life cycle, so the adult insecticide is used to kill the newly hatched adult fleas before they find a host. Most IGRs are active for many months, while

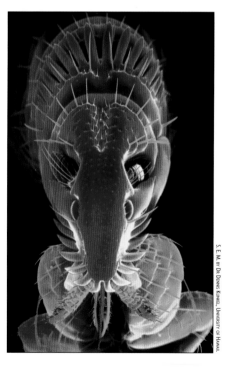

A scanning electron micrograph of a dog or cat flea, *Ctenocephalides*, magnified more than 100x. This image has been colorized for effect.

THE LIFE CYCLE OF THE FLEA

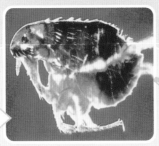

Adult

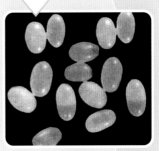

Egg

**Pupa
or
Nymph**

Larva

Fleas have been around for millions of years and have adapted to changing host animals. They are able to go through a complete life cycle in less than one month or they can extend their lives to almost two years by remaining as pupae or cocoons. They do not need blood or any other food for up to 20 months.

INSECT GROWTH REGULATOR (IGR)

Two types of products should be used when treating fleas—a product to treat the pet and a product to treat the home. Adult fleas represent less than 1% of the flea population. The pre-adult fleas (eggs, larvae and pupae) represent more than 99% of the flea population and are found in the environment; it is in the case of pre-adult fleas that products containing an Insect Growth Regulator (IGR) should be used in the home.

IGRs are a new class of compounds used to prevent the development of insects. They do not kill the insect outright, but instead use the insect's biology against it to stop it from completing its growth. Products that contain methoprene are the world's first and leading IGRs. Used to control fleas and other insects, this type of IGR will stop flea larvae from developing and protect the house for up to seven months.

The American dog tick, *Dermacentor variabilis*, is probably the most common tick found on dogs. Look at the strength in its eight legs! No wonder it's hard to detach them.

adult insecticides are only active for a few days.

When treating with a household spray, it is a good idea to vacuum before applying the product. This stimulates as many pupae as possible to hatch into adult fleas. The vacuum cleaner should also be treated with an insecticide to prevent the eggs and larvae that have been collected in the vacuum bag from hatching.

The second stage of treatment is to apply an adult insecticide to the dog. Traditionally, this would be in the form of a collar or a spray, but more recent innovations include digestible insecticides that poison the fleas when they ingest the dog's blood. Alternatively, there are drops that, when placed on the back of the dog's neck, spread throughout the dog's hair and skin to kill adult fleas.

TICKS

Though not as common as fleas, ticks are found all over the tropical and temperate world. They don't bite, like fleas; they harpoon. They dig their sharp proboscis (nose) into the dog's skin and drink the blood. Their

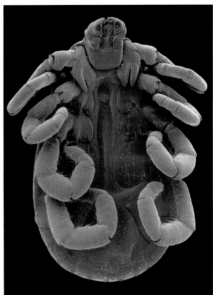

S. E. M. BY DR. DENNIS KUNKEL, UNIVERSITY OF HAWAII.

only food and drink is dog's blood. Dogs can get Lyme disease, Rocky Mountain spotted fever, tick bite paralysis and many other diseases from ticks. They may live where fleas are found and they like to hide in cracks or seams in walls. They are controlled the same way fleas are controlled.

The American dog tick, *Dermacentor variabilis*, may well be the most common dog tick in many geographical areas, especially those areas where the climate is hot and humid. Most dog ticks have life expectancies of a week to six months, depending upon climatic conditions. They can neither jump nor fly, but they can crawl slowly and can range up to 16 feet to reach a sleeping or unsuspecting dog.

MITES

Just as fleas and ticks can be problematic for your dog, mites can also lead to an itchy nuisance. Microscopic in size, mites are related to ticks and generally take up permanent residence on their host animal— in this case, your dog! The term *mange* refers to any infestation caused by one of the mighty mites, of which there are six varieties that concern dog owners.

Demodex mites cause a condition known as demodicosis

DEER-TICK CROSSING

The great outdoors may be fun for your dog, but it also is an home to dangerous ticks. Deer ticks carry a bacterium known as *Borrelia burgdorferi* and are most active in the autumn and spring. When infections are caught early, penicillin and tetracycline are effective antibiotics, but, if left untreated, the bacteria may cause neurological, kidney and cardiac problems as well as long-term trouble with walking and painful joints.

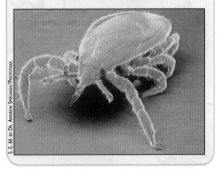

S. E. M. BY DR. ANDREW SPIELMAN/PHOTOTAKE.

PHOTO BY DR. DENNIS KUNKEL, UNIVERSITY OF HAWAII.

The head of an American dog tick, *Dermacentor variabilis*, enlarged and colorized for effect.

127

The mange mite, *Psoroptes bovis*, can infest cattle and other domestic animals.

PHOTO BY JAMES HAYDEN/YOAV/PHOTOTAKE.

(sometimes called red mange or follicular mange), in which the mites live in the dog's hair follicles and sebaceous glands. This type of mange is commonly passed from the dam to her puppies and usually shows up on the puppies' muzzles, though demodicosis is not transferable from one normal dog to another. Most dogs recover from this type of mange without any treatment, though topical therapies are commonly prescribed by the vet.

The *Cheyletiellosis* mite is the hook-mouthed culprit associated with "walking dandruff," a condition that affects dogs as well as cats and rabbits. This mite lives on the surface of the animal's skin and is readily transferable through direct or indirect contact with an affected animal. The dandruff is present in the form of scaly skin, which may or may not be itchy. If not treated, this mange can affect a whole kennel of dogs and can be spread to humans as well.

The *Sarcoptes* mite causes intense itching on the dog in the form of a condition known as scabies or sarcoptic mange. The cycle of the *Sarcoptes* mite lasts about three weeks, and the mites live in the top layer of the dog's skin (epidermis), preferably in

Human lice look like dog lice; the two are closely related.

PHOTO BY DWIGHT R. KUHN.

areas with little hair. Scabies is highly contagious and can be passed to humans. Sometimes an allergic reaction to the mite worsens the severe itching associated with sarcoptic mange.

Ear mites, *Otodectes cynotis,* lead to otodectic mange, which most commonly affects the outer ear canal of the dog, though other areas can be affected as well. Dogs with ear-mite infestation commonly scratch at their ears, causing further irritation, and shake their heads. Dark brown droppings in the outer ear confirm the diagnosis. Your vet can prescribe a treatment to flush out the ears and kill any eggs in the ears. A complete month of treatment is necessary to cure the mange.

Two other mites, less common in dogs, include *Dermanyssus gallinae* (the poultry or red mite) and *Eutrombicula alfreddugesi* (the North American mite associated with trombiculidiasis or chigger infestation). The poultry mite frequently lives on chickens, but can transfer to dogs who spend time near farm animals. Chigger infestation affects dogs in the

DO NOT MIX
Never mix parasite-control products without first consulting your vet. Some products can become toxic when combined with others and can cause fatal consequences.

NOT A DROP TO DRINK
Never allow your dog to swim in polluted water or public areas where water quality can be suspect. Even perfectly clear water can harbor parasites, many of which can cause serious to fatal illnesses in canines. Areas inhabited by water-fowl and other wildlife are especially dangerous.

central US who have exposure to woodlands. The types of mange caused by both of these mites are treatable by veterinarians.

INTERNAL PARASITES

Most animals—fishes, birds and mammals, including dogs and humans—have worms and other parasites that live inside their bodies. According to Dr. Herbert R. Axelrod, the fish pathologist, there are two kinds of parasites: dumb and smart. The smart parasites live in peaceful cooperation with their hosts (symbiosis), while the dumb parasites kill their hosts. Most worm infections are relatively easy to control. If they are not controlled, they weaken the host dog to the point that other medical problems occur, but they do not kill the host as dumb parasites would.

A brown dog tick, *Rhipicephalus sanguineus*, is an uncommon but annoying tick found on dogs.

PHOTO BY CAROLINA BIOLOGICAL SUPPLY/PHOTOTAKE.

129

The roundworm *Rhabditis* can infect both dogs and humans.

The roundworm, *Ascaris lumbricoides*.

ROUNDWORMS

Average-size dogs can pass 1,360,000 roundworm eggs every day. For example, if there were only 1 million dogs in the world, the world would be saturated with thousands of tons of dog feces. These feces would contain around 15,000,000,000 roundworm eggs.

Up to 31% of home yards and children's sand boxes in the US contain roundworm eggs.

Flushing dog's feces down the toilet is not a safe practice because the usual sewage treatments do not destroy roundworm eggs.

Infected puppies start shedding roundworm eggs at three weeks of age. They can be infected by their mother's milk.

ROUNDWORMS

The roundworms that infect dogs are known scientifically as *Toxocara canis*. They live in the dog's intestines and shed eggs continually. It has been estimated that a dog produces about 6 or more ounces of feces every day. Each ounce of feces averages hundreds of thousands of roundworm eggs. There are no known areas in which dogs roam that do not contain roundworm eggs. The greatest danger of roundworms is that they infect people, too! It is wise to have your dog tested regularly for roundworms.

In young puppies, roundworms cause bloated bellies, diarrhea, coughing and vomiting, and are transmitted from the dam (through blood or milk). Affected puppies will not appear as animated as normal puppies. The worms appear spaghetti-like, measuring as long as 6 inches. Adult dogs can acquire roundworms through coprophagia (eating contaminated feces) or by killing rodents that carry roundworms.

Roundworm infection can kill puppies and cause severe problems in adults, as the hatched larvae travel to the lungs and trachea through the bloodstream. Cleanliness is the best preventative for roundworms. Always pick up after your dog and dispose of feces in appropriate receptacles.

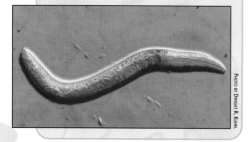

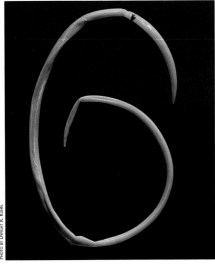

PHOTO BY DWIGHT R. KUHL.

HOOKWORMS

In the United States, dog owners have to be concerned about four different species of hookworm, the most common and most serious of which is *Ancylostoma caninum,* which prefers warm climates. The others are *Ancylostoma braziliense, Ancylostoma tubaeforme* and *Uncinaria stenocephala,* the latter of which is a concern to dogs living in the northern US and Canada, as this species prefers cold climates. Hookworms are dangerous to humans as well as to dogs and cats, and can be the cause of severe anemia due to iron deficiency. The worm uses its teeth to attach itself to the dog's intestines and changes the site of its attachment about six times per day. Each time the worm repositions itself, the dog loses blood and can become anemic. *Ancylostoma caninum* is the most likely of the four species to cause anemia in the dog.

Symptoms of hookworm infection include dark stools, weight loss, general weakness, pale coloration and anemia, as well as possible skin problems. Fortunately, hookworms are easily purged from the affected dog with a number of medications that have proven effective. Discuss these with your veterinarian. Most heartworm preventatives include a hookworm insecticide as well.

Owners also must be aware that hookworms can infect humans, who can acquire the larvae through exposure to contaminated feces. Since the worms cannot complete their life cycle on a human, the worms simply infest the skin and cause irritation. This condition is known as cutaneous larva migrans syndrome. As a preventative, use disposable gloves or a "poop-scoop" to pick up your dog's droppings and prevent your dog (or neighborhood cats) from defecating in children's play areas.

The hookworm *Ancylostoma caninum.*

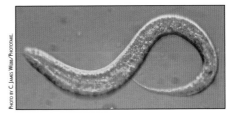

PHOTO BY C. JAMES WEBB/PHOTOTAKE.

The infective stage of the hookworm larva.

131

TAPEWORMS

Humans, rats, squirrels, foxes, coyotes, wolves and domestic dogs are all susceptible to tapeworm infection. Except in humans, tapeworms are usually not a fatal infection. Infected individuals can harbor 1000 parasitic worms.

Tapeworms, like some other types of worm, are hermaphroditic, meaning male and female in the same worm.

If dogs eat infected rats or mice, or anything else infected with tapeworm, they get the tapeworm disease. One month after attaching to a dog's intestine, the worm starts shedding eggs. These eggs are infective immediately. Infective eggs can live for a few months without a host animal.

The head and rostellum (the round prominence on the scolex) of a tapeworm, which infects dogs and humans.

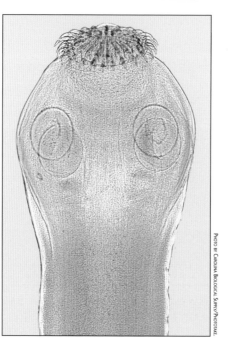

PHOTO BY CAROLINA BIOLOGICAL SUPPLY/PHOTOTAKE.

TAPEWORMS

There are many species of tapeworm, all of which are carried by fleas! The most common tapeworm affecting dogs is known as *Dipylidium caninum*. The dog eats the flea and starts the tapeworm cycle. Humans can also be infected with tapeworms—so don't eat fleas! Fleas are so small that your dog could pass them onto your hands, your plate or your food and thus make it possible for you to ingest a flea that is carrying tapeworm eggs.

While tapeworm infection is not life-threatening in dogs (smart parasite!), it can be the cause of a very serious liver disease for humans. About 50% of the humans infected with *Echinococcus multilocularis*, a type of tapeworm that causes alveolar hydatid, perish.

WHIPWORMS

In North America, whipworms are counted among the most common parasitic worms in dogs. The whipworm's scientific name is *Trichuris vulpis*. These worms attach themselves in the lower parts of the intestine, where they feed. Affected dogs may only experience upset tummies, colic and diarrhea. These worms, however, can live for months or years in the dog, beginning their larval stage in the small intestine, spending their adult stage in the large intestine and finally passing infective eggs through the dog's feces. The only way to detect whipworms is through a fecal examination, though this is not always foolproof. Treatment for whipworms is tricky, due to the worms' unusual life-cycle pattern, and very often dogs are reinfected due to exposure to infective eggs on the ground. The whipworm eggs can survive in the environment for as long as five years, thus cleaning up droppings in your own backyard as well as in public places is absolutely essential for sanitation purposes and the health of your dog.

THREADWORMS

Though less common than roundworms, hookworms and those mentioned above, threadworms concern dog owners in the southwestern US and Gulf Coast area, where the climate is hot and humid. Living in the small intestine of the dog, this worm measures a mere 2 millimeters and is round in shape. Like that of the whipworm, the threadworm's life cycle is very complex and the eggs and larvae are passed through the feces. A deadly disease in humans, *Strongyloides* readily infects people, and the handling of feces is the most common means of transmission. Threadworms are most often seen in young puppies; bloody diarrhea and pneumonia are symptoms. Sick puppies must be isolated and treated immediately; vets recommend a follow-up treatment one month later.

HEARTWORM PREVENTATIVES

There are many heartworm preventatives on the market, many of which are sold at your veterinarian's office. These products can be given daily or monthly, depending on the manufacturer's instructions. All of these preventatives contain chemical insecticides directed at killing heartworms, which leads to some controversy among dog owners. In effect, heartworm preventatives are necessary evils, though you should determine how necessary based on your pet's lifestyle. There is no doubt that heartworm is a dreadful disease that threatens the lives of dogs. However, the likelihood of your dog's being bitten by an infected mosquito is slim in most places, and a mosquito-repellent (or an herbal remedy such as Wormwood or Black Walnut) is much safer for your dog and will not compromise his immune system (the way heartworm preventatives will). Should you decide to use the traditional preventative "medications," you can consider giving the pill every other or third month. Since the toxins in the pill will kill the heartworms at all stages of development, the pill would be effective in killing larvae, nymphs or adults and it takes four months for the larvae to reach the adult stage. Thus, there is no rationale to poisoning the dog's system on a monthly basis. Lastly, do not give the pill during the winter months since there are no mosquitoes around to pass on their infection, unless you live in a tropical environment.

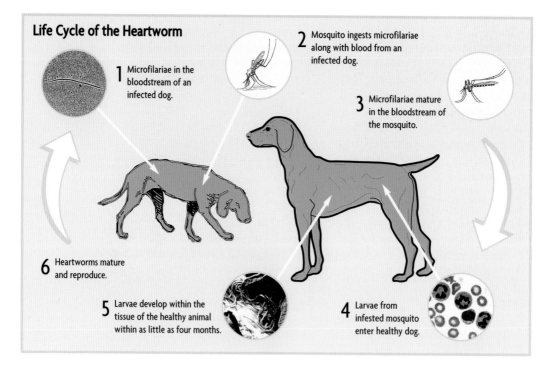

Life Cycle of the Heartworm

1 Microfilariae in the bloodstream of an infected dog.

2 Mosquito ingests microfilariae along with blood from an infected dog.

3 Microfilariae mature in the bloodstream of the mosquito.

6 Heartworms mature and reproduce.

5 Larvae develop within the tissue of the healthy animal within as little as four months.

4 Larvae from infested mosquito enter healthy dog.

HEARTWORMS

Heartworms are thin, extended worms up to 12 inches long, which live in a dog's heart and the major blood vessels surrounding it. Dogs may have up to 200 worms. Symptoms may be loss of energy, loss of appetite, coughing, the development of a pot belly and anemia.

Heartworms are transmitted by mosquitoes. The mosquito drinks the blood of an infected dog and takes in larvae with the blood. The larvae, called microfilariae, develop within the body of the mosquito and are passed on to the next dog bitten after the larvae mature. It takes two to three weeks for the larvae to develop to the infective stage within the body of the mosquito. Dogs are usually treated at about six weeks of age and maintained on a prophylactic dose given monthly.

Blood testing for heartworms is not necessarily indicative of how seriously your dog is infected. Although this is a dangerous disease, it is not easy for a dog to be infected. Discuss the various preventatives with your vet, as there are many different types now available. Together you can decide on a safe course of prevention for your dog.

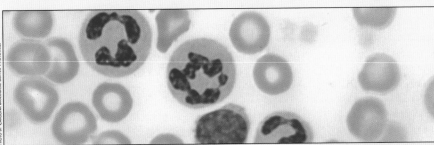

Magnified heart-
worm larvae,
Dirofilaria immitis.

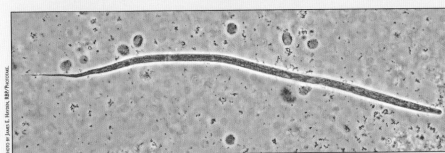

Heartworm,
*Dirofilaria
immitis.*

The heart
of a dog infected
with canine heart-
worm, *Dirofilaria
immitis.*

BREED-RELATED HEREDITARY CONDITIONS

HIP DYSPLASIA

This is a congenital problem whereby the acetabulum (hip socket), into which the femoral head (knucklebone) rests, degenerates. It can only be diagnosed by scrutiny of an x-ray by specialists trained to do so. The Orthopedic Foundation for Animals (OFA), the worlds' largest data bank on hip status x-rays, is dedicated to establishing control programs to lower the incidence of hip dysplasia in pure-bred dogs. The x-rays of Springers over 24 months of age are reviewed by a three board-certified veterinary radiologists, whose consensus determines the scoring of the hips. OFA numbers are assigned to those scores of "Excellent," "Good" and "Fair." Hips that are designated "Borderline," "Mild," "Moderate" and "Severe" are ineligible for an OFA number. Most breeders x-ray all the dogs they use for breeding and eliminate those dogs with a high hip score from their breeding programs.

The OFA also registers carriers of elbow dysplasia, craniomandibular osteopathy (CM), osteochondritis dessicans (OCD), ununited anchoneal process and other heritable diseases.

PROGRESSIVE RETINAL ATROPHY (PRA)

PRA is a congenital disease of the eye that is causing much concern

DO YOU KNOW ABOUT HIP DYSPLASIA?

Hip dysplasia is a fairly common condition found in pure-bred dogs. When a dog has hip dysplasia, his hind leg has an incorrectly formed hip joint. By constant use of the hip joint, it becomes more and more loose, wears abnormally and may become arthritic.

Hip dysplasia can only be confirmed with an x-ray, but certain symptoms may indicate a problem. Your dog may have a hip dysplasia problem if he walks in a peculiar manner, hops instead of smoothly runs, uses his hind legs in unison (to keep the pressure off the weak joint), has trouble getting up from a prone position or always sits with both legs together on one side of his body.

As the dog matures, he may adapt well to life with a bad hip, but in a few years the arthritis develops and many dogs with hip dysplasia become cripples.

Hip dysplasia is considered an inherited disease and can usually be diagnosed when the dog is three to nine months old. Some experts claim that a special diet might help your puppy outgrow the bad hip, but the usual treatments are surgical. The removal of the pectineus muscle, the removal of the round part of the femur, reconstructing the pelvis and replacing the hip with an artificial one are all surgical interventions that are expensive, but they are usually very successful. Follow the advice of your veterinarian.

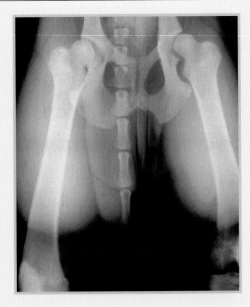

HIP DYSPLASIA

Compare the two hip joints and you'll understand dysplasia better. Hip dysplasia is a badly worn hip joint caused by inproper fit of the bone into the socket.

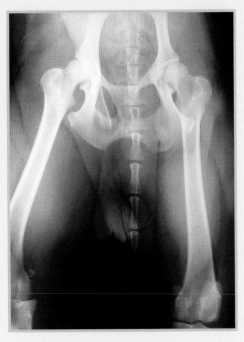

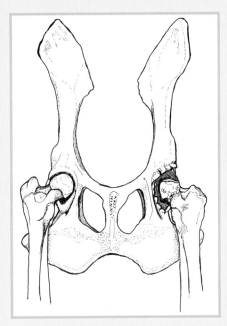

The illustration shows a healthy hip joint on the left and an unhealthy hip joint on the right.

Hip dysplasia can only be positively diagnosed by x-ray. English Springer Spaniels can manifest the problem when they are puppies, during the so-called fast growth period but a dog can only be definitively diagnosed with or cleared as free of hip dysplasia once he has reached two years of age.

Springers love to swim, but should not be allowed in water that appears polluted. Harmful bacteria, which can cause your dog to become sick, are sometimes found in lakes and ponds.

Opposite page: A scanning electron micrograph image of typical dog hairs, enlarged 600 times. These are healthy hairs, evidenced by the cuticles' being neat and uniform. SEM by Dr. Dennis Kunkel, University of Hawaii.

in canine circles. It is inherited through a recessive gene, i.e., both parents must be carriers of the gene to produce affected offspring. The symptoms rarely manifest themselves until a dog is mature, sometimes even at six or seven years of age, so that the dog or bitch may well have been used for breeding. The disease can only be diagnosed by a specialist with special equipment. In many countries, eye testing is obligatory if one wants to breed and the results of the eye tests are published in a veterinary dog journal.

CATARACTS
Cataracts are a condition whereby the lens of the eyes becomes covered with a milky film and the dog's eyesight is seriously affected. It is often found in older dogs. However, cataracts can also be inherited and affect young Springers. Dogs that are being tested for PRA will normally also be tested for cataracts. Contrary to

PRA, cataracts can occur in one eye only.

RETINAL DYSPLASIA (RD)
RD in its simplest form is seen as a multiple folding of the retina, while the most severe form is non-attachment of the retina to the underlying choroid. The effect on sight varies from no apparent effect to total blindness. Testing on RD can be done in the litter, although the test, the same as the tests on PRA and cataracts, has to be repeated annually.

CANINE FUCOSIDOSIS
This disease was first noticed in 1980 in Australia where both English Springers and humans were affected. Affected dogs show loss of weight, increasing wobbliness of gait, odd muscle spasms and increasing difficulty in eating. There is no known cure for the disease but it can be diagnosed easily. The cause is a deficiency of a certain enzyme or chemical that is essential for the breakdown of a sugar (fucose) in body cells. Affected dogs are born without the gene that produces this enzyme. A blood test can determine whether a dog is a carrier for this disease. Responsible breeders have been very careful in their breeding and have gotten the problem under control. Affected dogs suffer emaciation, neurological defects and cerebral degeneration within the first two years of life.

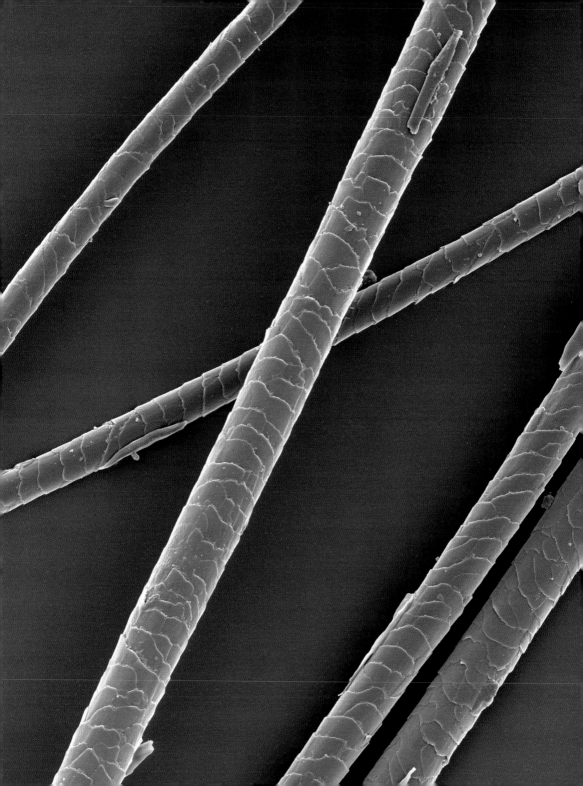

Your Senior
ENGLISH SPRINGER SPANIEL

The term *old* is a qualitative term. For dogs, as well as their masters, old is relative. Certainly we can all distinguish between a puppy English Springer Spaniel and an adult Springer—there are the obvious physical traits, such as size, appearance and facial expressions, and personality traits. Puppies and young dogs like to play with children. Children's natural exuberance is a good match for the seemingly endless energy of young dogs. They like to run, jump, chase and retrieve. When dogs grow up and cease their interaction with children, they are often thought of as being too old to play with the kids.

On the other hand, if an English Springer Spaniel is only exposed to people with quieter lifestyles, his life will normally be less active and he will not seem to be getting old as his activity level slows down.

If people live to be 100 years old, dogs live to be 20 years old. While this is a good rule of thumb, it is very inaccurate. When trying to compare dog years to human years, you cannot make a generalization about all dogs. You can make the generalization that 13 years is a good lifespan for an English Springer Spaniel, which is quite good compared to many other purebred dogs that may only live to eight or nine years of age. Some Springers have been known to live to 17 or more years. Dogs are generally considered mature within three years, but they can reproduce even earlier. So the first three years of a dog's life are like seven times that of comparable humans. That means a 3-year-old dog is like a 21-year-old human. As the curve of comparison shows, there is no hard and fast rule for comparing dog and human ages. The comparison is made even more difficult, for not all humans age at the same rate...and human females live longer than human males.

GETTING OLD

The bottom line is simply that your dog is getting old when you think he is getting old because he slows down in his level of general activity, including walking, running, eating, jumping and retrieving. On the other hand, the frequency of certain activities increases, such as more sleeping, more barking and more repetition of habits like going to the door without being called when you put your coat on to leave the house.

WHAT TO LOOK FOR IN SENIORS

Most veterinarians and behaviorists use the seven-year mark as the time to consider a dog a senior. The term *senior* does not imply that the dog is geriatric and has begun to fail in mind and body. Aging is essentially a slowing process. Humans readily admit that they feel a difference in their activity level from age 20 to 30, and then from 30 to 40, etc. By treating the seven-year-old dog as a senior, owners are able to implement certain therapeutic and preventative medical strategies with the help of their veterinarians. A senior-care program should include at least two veterinary visits per year, screening sessions to determine the dog's health status, as well as nutritional counseling. Veterinarians determine the senior dog's health status through a blood smear for a complete blood count, serum chemistry profile with electrolytes, urinalysis, blood pressure check, electrocardiogram, ocular tonometry (pressure on the eyeball) and dental prophylaxis.

Such an extensive program for senior dogs is well advised before owners start to see the obvious physical signs of aging, such as slower and inhibited movement, graying, increased sleep/nap periods and disinterest in play and other activity. This preventative program promises a longer, healthier life for the aging dog. Among the physical problems common in aging dogs are the loss of hearing and vision, arthritis, kidney and liver failure, diabetes

mellitus, heart disease and Cushing's disease (a hormonal disease).

In addition to the physical manifestations discussed, there are some behavioral changes and problems related to aging dogs. Dogs suffering from hearing or vision loss, dental discomfort or arthritis can become aggressive. Likewise the near-deaf and/or blind dog may be startled more easily and react in an unexpect-

As your Springer gets older, do not expect that he will maintain the same level of energy and activity.

edly aggressive manner. Seniors suffering from senility can become more impatient and irritable. Housesoiling accidents are associated with loss of mobility, kidney problems, loss of sphincter control as well as plaque accumulation, physiological brain changes and reactions to medications. Older dogs, just like young puppies, suffer from separation anxiety, which can lead to excessive barking, whining, housesoiling and destructive behavior. Seniors may become fearful of everyday sounds, such as vacuum cleaners, heaters, thunder and passing traffic. Some dogs have difficulty sleeping, due to discomfort, the need for frequent bathroom visits and the like. Owners should avoid spoiling the older dog with too many fatty treats. Obesity is a common problem in older dogs and subtracts years from their lives. Keep the senior dog as trim as possible since excessive weight puts additional stress on the body's vital organs. Some breeders recommend supplementing the diet with foods high in fiber and lower in calories. Adding fresh vegetables and marrow broth to the senior's diet makes a tasty, low-calorie, low-fat supplement. Vets also offer specialty diets for senior dogs that are worth exploring.

Your dog, as he nears his twilight years, needs his owner's patience and good care more than

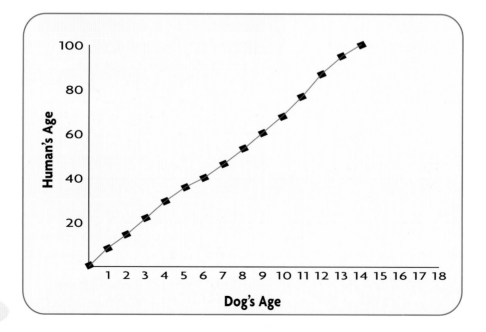

WHEN YOUR DOG GETS OLD...
SIGNS THE OWNER CAN LOOK FOR

IF YOU NOTICE...	IT COULD INDICATE...
Discoloration of teeth and gums, foul breath, loss of appetite	Abcesses, gum disease, mouth lesions
Lumps, bumps, cysts, warts, fatty tumors	Cancers, benign or malignant
Cloudiness of eyes, apparent loss of sight	Cataracts, lenticular sclerosis, PRA, retinal dysplasia, blindness
Flaky coat, alopecia (hair loss)	Hormonal problems, hypothyroidism
Obesity, appetite loss, excessive weight gain	Various problems
Household accidents, increased urination	Diabetes, kidney or bladder disease
Increased thirst	Kidney disease, diabetes mellitus, bladder infection
Change in sleeping habits, coughing	Heart disease
Difficulty moving	Arthritis, degenerative joint disease, spondylosis (degenerative spine disease)

IF YOU NOTICE ANY OF THESE SIGNS, AN APPOINTMENT SHOULD BE MADE IMMEDIATELY WITH A VET FOR A THOROUGH EVALUATION.

ever. Never punish an older dog for an accident or abnormal behavior. For all the years of love, protection and companionship that your dog has provided, he deserves special attention and courtesies. The older dog may need to relieve himself at 3 a.m. because he can no longer hold it for eight hours. Older dogs may not be able to remain crated for more than two or three hours. It may be time to give up a sofa or chair to your old friend. Although he may not seem as enthusiastic about your attention and petting, he does appreciate the considerations you offer as he gets older.

Your English Springer Spaniel does not understand why his world is slowing down. Owners must make the transition into the golden years as pleasant and rewarding as possible.

WHAT TO DO WHEN THE TIME COMES

You are never fully prepared to make a rational decision about putting your dog to sleep. It is very obvious that you love your English Springer Spaniel or you would not be reading this book. Putting a loved dog to sleep is extremely difficult. It is a decision that must be made with your veterinarian. You are usually forced to make the decision when one of the life-threatening symptoms listed above becomes serious enough for you to seek veterinary help.

If the prognosis of the malady indicates the end is near and your beloved pet will only suffer more and experience no enjoyment for the balance of his life, then euthanasia is the right choice.

WHAT IS EUTHANASIA?

Euthanasia derives from the Greek, meaning *good death*. In other words, it means the planned, painless killing of a dog suffering from a painful, incurable condition, or who is so aged that he cannot walk, see, eat or control his excretory functions.

Euthanasia is usually accomplished by injection with an overdose of an anesthesia or barbiturate. Aside from the prick of the needle, the experience is usually painless.

MAKING THE DECISION

The decision to euthanize your dog is never easy. The days during which the dog becomes ill and the end occurs can be unusually stressful for you. If this is your first experience with the death of a loved one, you may need the comfort dictated by your religious beliefs. If you are the head of the family and have children, you should have involved them in the decision of putting your English Springer Spaniel to sleep. Usually your dog can be maintained on drugs

CDS: COGNITIVE DYSFUNCTION SYNDROME
"Old-Dog Syndrome"

There are many ways for you to evaluate old-dog syndrome. Veterinarians have defined CDS (cognitive dysfunction syndrome) as the gradual deterioration of cognitive abilities. These are indicated by changes in the dog's behavior. When a dog changes his routine response, and maladies have been eliminated as the cause of these behavioral changes, then CDS is the usual diagnosis.

More than half the dogs over eight years old suffer from some form of CDS. The older the dog, the more chance he has of suffering from CDS. In humans, doctors often dismiss the CDS behavioral changes as part of "winding down."

There are four major signs of CDS: frequent housebreaking accidents inside the home, sleeps much more or much less than normal, acts confused, and fails to respond to social stimuli.

SYMPTOMS OF CDS

FREQUENT POTTY ACCIDENTS
- *Urinates in the house.*
- *Defecates in the house.*
- *Doesn't signal that he wants to go out.*

SLEEP PATTERNS
- *Moves much more slowly.*
- *Sleeps more than normal during the day.*
- *Sleeps less during the night.*

CONFUSION
- *Walks around listlessly and without a destination goal.*
- *Goes outside and just stands there.*
- *Appears confused with a faraway look in his eyes.*
- *Hides more often.*
- *Doesn't recognize friends.*
- *Doesn't come when called.*

FAILS TO RESPOND TO SOCIAL STIMULI
- *Comes to people less frequently, whether called or not.*
- *Doesn't tolerate petting for more than a short time.*
- *Doesn't come to the door when you return home from work.*

for a few days in order to give you ample time to make a decision. During this time, talking with members of your family or even people who have lived through this same experience can ease the burden of your inevitable decision.

THE FINAL RESTING PLACE

Dogs can have some of the same privileges as humans. They can occasionally be buried in their entirety in a pet cemetery which is generally expensive, or they can be buried in your yard in a place suitably marked with some stone or newly planted tree or bush. Alternatively they can be cremated and the ashes returned to you, or some people prefer to leave their dogs at the vet's office for the vet to dispose of.

All of these options should be discussed frankly and openly with your veterinarian. Do not be afraid to ask financial questions. Cremations can be individual, but a less expensive option is mass cremation, although of course the ashes can not then be returned. Vets can usually arrange cremation services on your behalf.

GETTING ANOTHER DOG?

The grief of losing your beloved dog will be as lasting as the grief of losing a human friend or relative. In most cases, if your dog died of old age (if there is such a thing), he had slowed down considerably. Do you want a new Springer puppy to replace him? Or are you better off in finding a more mature Springer, say two to three years of age, which will usually be house-trained and will have an already developed personality. In this case, you can find out if you like each other after a few hours of being together.

The decision is, of course, your own. Do you want another English Springer Spaniel or perhaps a different breed so as to avoid comparison with your beloved friend? Most people usually buy the same breed because they know and love the characteristics of that breed. Then, too, they often know people who have the same breed and perhaps they are lucky enough that a breeder they know and respect expects a litter soon. What could be better?

Pet cemeteries offer suitable receptacles for dogs' ashes.

Showing Your
ENGLISH SPRINGER SPANIEL

When you purchase your English Springer Spaniel, you will make it clear to the breeder whether you want one just as a lovable companion and pet, or if you hope to be buying an English Springer Spaniel with show prospects. No reputable breeder will sell you a young puppy and tell you that it is definitely of show quality, for so much can go wrong during the early months of a puppy's development. If you plan to show, what you will hopefully have acquired is a puppy with "show potential."

To the novice, exhibiting an English Springer Spaniel in the show ring may look easy, but it takes a lot of hard work and devotion to do top winning at a show such as the prestigious Westminster Kennel Club dog show, not to mention a little luck too!

The first concept that the canine novice learns when watching a dog show is that each dog first competes against members of his own breed. Once the judge has selected the best member of each breed (Best of Breed), that chosen dog will compete with other dogs in his group. Finally, the dogs chosen first in each group will compete for Best in Show.

The second concept that you must understand is that the dogs are not actually compared against one another. The judge compares each dog against his breed standard, the written description of

Dog shows are exciting opportunities to meet other Springer enthusiasts and to learn more about this wonderful breed.

and judges would never agree that it was indeed "perfect.")

If you are interested in exploring the world of dog showing, your best bet is to join your local breed club or the national parent club, which is the English Springer Spaniel Club Field Trial Association. These clubs often host both regional and national specialties, shows only for English Springer Spaniels, which can include conformation as well as obedience, agility and field trials. Even if you have no intention of competing with your Springer, a specialty is like a festival for lovers of the breed who congregate to share their favorite topic: Springers! Clubs also send out newsletters, and some organize training days and seminars in order that people may learn more about their chosen breed. To locate the breed club closest to you, contact the AKC, which furnishes the rules and regulations for all of these events plus general dog registration and other basic requirements of dog ownership.

The American Kennel Club offers three kinds of conformation shows: an all-breed show (for all AKC-recognized breeds), a specialty show (for one breed only, usually sponsored by the parent club) and a Group show (for all breeds in the Group).

For a dog to become an AKC champion of record, the dog must

The Springer's movement in the show ring, as described in the AKC breed standard, should be smooth and effortless, never high-stepping or with a short, choppy stride.

the ideal specimen that is approved by the American Kennel Club (AKC). While some early breed standards were indeed based on specific dogs that were famous or popular, many dedicated enthusiasts say that a perfect specimen, as described in the standard, has never walked into a show ring, has never been bred and, to the woe of dog breeders around the globe, does not exist. Breeders attempt to get as close to this ideal as possible with every litter, but theoretically the "perfect" dog is so elusive that it is impossible. (And if the "perfect" dog were born, breeders

accumulate 15 points at the shows from at least three different judges, including two "majors." A "major" is defined as a three-, four- or five-point win, and the number of points per win is determined on the number of dogs entered in the show on the day. Depending on the breed, the number of points that are awarded varies. In a breed as popular as the English Springer Spaniel, more dogs are needed to rack up the points. At any dog show, only one dog and one bitch of each breed can win points.

Dog showing does not offer "co-ed" classes. Dogs and bitches never compete against each other in the classes. Non-champion dogs are called "class dogs" because they compete in one of five classes. Dogs are entered in a particular class depending on his age and previous show wins. To begin, there is the Puppy Class (for 6- to 9-month-olds and for 9- to 12-month-olds); this class is followed by the Novice Class (for dogs that have not won any first prizes except in the Puppy Class or three first prizes in the Novice Class and have not accumulated any points toward their champion title); the Bred-by-Exhibitor Class (for dogs handled by their breeders or handled by one of the breeder's immediate family); the American-bred Class (for dogs bred in the US); and the Open Class (for any dog that is not a champion).

The judge at the show begins judging the Puppy Class, first dogs and then bitches, and proceeds through the classes. The judge places his winners first through fourth in each class. In the Winners Class, the first-place winners of each class compete with one another to determine Winners Dog and Winners Bitch. The judge also places a Reserve Winners Dog and Reserve Winners Bitch, which could be awarded the points in the case of a disqualification. The Winners Dog and Winners Bitch, the two that are awarded the points for the breed, then compete with any champions of record entered in the show. The judge reviews the Winners Dog, Winners Bitch and all the other champions to select his Best of Breed. The Best of Winners is selected between the Winners Dog and Winners Bitch. Were one of these two to be selected Best of Breed, it would automatically be named Best of Winners as well. Finally the judge selects his Best of Opposite Sex to the Best of Breed winner.

At a Group show or all-breed show, the Best of Breed winners from each breed then compete against one another for Group One through Group Four. The judge compares each Best of Breed to his breed standard, and the dog that most closely lives up to the ideal for his breed is selected as Group One. Finally, all seven group winners (from the Sporting Group, Toy Group, Hound Group, etc.) compete for Best in Show.

To find out about dog shows in your area, you can subscribe to the American Kennel Club's monthly magazine, *The American Kennel Gazette* and the accompanying *Events Calendar*. You can also look in your local newspaper for advertisements for dog shows in your area or go on the Internet to the AKC's website, www.akc.org.

If your English Springer Spaniel is six months of age or older and registered with the AKC, you can enter him in a dog show where the breed is offered classes. Provided that your English Springer Spaniel does not have a disqualifying fault, he can compete. Only unaltered dogs can be entered in a dog show, so if you have spayed or neutered your English Springer Spaniel, your dog cannot compete in conformation shows. The reason for this is simple. Dog shows are the main forum to prove which representatives in a breed are worthy of being bred. Only dogs that have achieved championships—the AKC "seal of approval" for quality in pure-bred dogs—should be bred. Altered dogs, however, can participate in other AKC events such as obedience trials and the Canine Good Citizen program.

Before you actually step into the ring, you would be well advised to sit back and observe the judge's ring procedure. The

A Springer is gaited by his handler as the judge evaluates the dog's movement.

A well-constructed Springer will exhibit a long, ground-covering stride, showing the proper development of the fore and hindquarters.

judge asks each handler to "stack" the dog, hopefully showing the dog off to his best advantage. The judge will observe the dog from a distance and from different angles, and approach the dog to check his teeth, overall structure, alertness and muscle tone, as well as consider how well the dog "conforms" to the standard. Most importantly, the judge will have the exhibitor move the dog around the ring in some pattern that he should specify. Finally, the judge will give the dog one last look before moving on to the next exhibitor.

If you are not in the top four in your class at your first show, do

INFORMATION ON CLUBS

You can get information about dog shows from the national kennel clubs:

American Kennel Club
5580 Centerview Dr., Raleigh, NC 27606-3390
www.akc.org

United Kennel Club
100 E. Kilgore Road, Kalamazoo, MI 49002
www.ukcdogs.com

Canadian Kennel Club
89 Skyway Ave., Suite 100, Etobicoke, Ontario
M9W 6R4 Canada
www.ckc.ca

The Kennel Club
1-5 Clarges St., Piccadilly, London W1Y 8AB, UK
www.the-kennel-club.org.uk

151

The Springer's natural instincts are tested in field trials.

not be discouraged. Be patient and consistent, and you may eventually find yourself in the winning line-up. Remember that the winners were once in your shoes and have devoted many hours and much money to earn the placement. If you find that your dog is losing every time and never getting a nod, it may be time to consider a different dog sport or to just enjoy your Springer as a pet. Parent clubs offer other events, such as agility, obedience, hunting tests and more, which may be of interest to the owner of a well-trained English Springer Spaniel.

FIELD TRIALS

Field trials are offered to the spaniel, retriever and pointer breeds of the Sporting Group as

The judge will open the Springer's mouth to evaluate the correct scissors bite.

well as some hound breeds. Spaniel field trials are geared to evaluate the performance of a trained hunting spaniel. The trial attempts to simulate what is expect in "an ordinary day's shooting," sometimes including water work as well as ground work. Open All-Age Stakes are recognized as the most important field trials and take a full day's time to run.

The judge evaluates each dog's ability to find and flush game eagerly, briskly and tacitly, while marking the fall or direction of the game and to retrieve it to hand. Steadiness to wing and shot is one of the most important qualifications of the working spaniel, as is the dog's ability to work with his handler and gun throughout the trial. AKC judges seek the following in spaniels at field trials:

- Control at all times, and under all conditions. Scenting ability and use of wind.
- Manner of covering ground and briskness of questing.
- Perseverance and courage in facing cover.
- Steadiness to flush, shot and command.
- Aptitude in marking fall of game and ability to find it.
- Ability and willingness to take hand signals.
- Promptness and style of retrieve and delivery.
- Proof of tender mouth.

An English Springer Spaniel can earn the titles of Field Champion or Amateur Field Champion once he has exhibited his ability to retrieve game from water after a swim. A water test can be held as a separate AKC-licensed event or in conjunction with a field trial.

HUNTING TESTS

Hunting tests are not competitive like field trials, and participating dogs are judged against a standard like in a conformation show. The intent of hunting tests is the same as that of field trials, to test the dog's ability in a simulated hunting scenario and to appreciate their dogs' natural innate ability in the field without the expense and pressure of a formal field trial.

The AKC instituted its hunting tests in June 1985 and popu-

larity has grown tremendously to include the spaniel and pointing breeds as well. The AKC offers three titles at hunting tests, Junior Hunter (JH), Senior Hunter (SH) and Master Hunter (MH). A JH spaniel must show the desire to hunt enthusiastically and fearlessly, obey basic whistle, hand and verbal commands and to flush and retrieve; a SH spaniel must exhibit boldness to cover and an intense desire to hunt, while maintaining a proper working distance and independent hunting sense; a MH spaniel must show keen enthusiasm and give a finished performance, always under the handler's control with an excellent ability to find game

The Springers' nose and natural gundog instincts are tested in hunting tests and field trials.

153

English Springer weaving through poles at an agility trial.

and be steady to wing and shot over land and water.

OBEDIENCE TRIALS

Obedience trials in the US trace back to the early 1930s when organized obedience training was developed to demonstrate how well dog and owner could work together. The pioneer of obedience trials is Mrs. Helen Whitehouse Walker, a Standard Poodle fancier, who designed a series of exercises after the Associated Sheep, Police Army Dog Society of Great Britain. Since the days of Mrs. Walker, obedience trials have grown by leaps and bounds, and today there are over 2,000 trials held in the US every year, with more than 100,000 dogs competing. Any AKC-registered dog can enter an obedience trial, regardless of conformational disqualifications or neutering.

Obedience trials are divided into three levels of progressive difficulty. At the first level, the Novice, dogs compete for the title Companion Dog (CD); at the intermediate level, the Open, dogs compete for the title Companion Dog Excellent (CDX); and at the advanced level, the Utility, dogs compete for the title Utility Dog (UD). Classes are sub-divided into "A" (for beginners) and "B" (for more experienced handlers). A perfect score at any level is 200, and a dog must score 170 or better to earn a "leg," of which three are

Taking the bar jump with grace and inches to spare at an agility trial.

needed to earn the title. To earn points, the dog must score more than 50% of the available points in each exercise; the possible points range from 20 to 40.

Each level consists of a different set of exercises. In the Novice level, the dog must heel on- and off-lead, come, long sit, long down and stand for examination. These skills are the basic ones required for a well-behaved "Companion Dog." The Open level requires that

the dog perform the same exercises above but without a leash for extended lengths of time, as well as retrieve a dumbbell, broad jump and drop on recall. In the Utility level, dogs must perform ten difficult exercises, including scent discrimination, hand signals for basic commands, directed jump and directed retrieve.

Once a dog has earned the UD title, he can compete with other proven obedience dogs for the coveted title of Utility Dog Excellent (UDX), which requires that the dog win "legs" in ten shows. Utility Dogs who earn "legs" in Open B and Utility B earn points toward their Obedience Trial Champion title. In 1977 the title Obedience Trial Champion (OTCh.) was established by the AKC. To become an OTCh., a dog needs to earn 100 points, which requires three first places in Open B and Utility under three different judges.

AGILITY TRIALS

Having had its origins in the UK back in 1977, AKC agility had its official beginning in the US in August 1994, when the first licensed agility trials were held. The AKC allows all registered breeds (including Miscellaneous Class breeds) to participate, providing the dog is 12 months of age or older. Agility is designed so that the handler demonstrates how well the dog can work at his

Retrieving a dumbbell at an agility trial is cinch for the well-trained Springer!

side. The handler directs his dog over an obstacle course that includes jumps as well as tires, the dog walk, weave poles, pipe tunnels, collapsed tunnels, etc. While working their way through the course, the dog must keep one eye and ear on the handler and the rest of his body on the course. The handler gives verbal and hand signals to guide the dog through the course.

Agility is great fun for dog and owner with many rewards for everyone involved. Interested owners should join a training club that has obstacles and experienced agility handlers who can introduce you and your dog to the "ropes" (and tires, tunnels, etc.).

INDEX

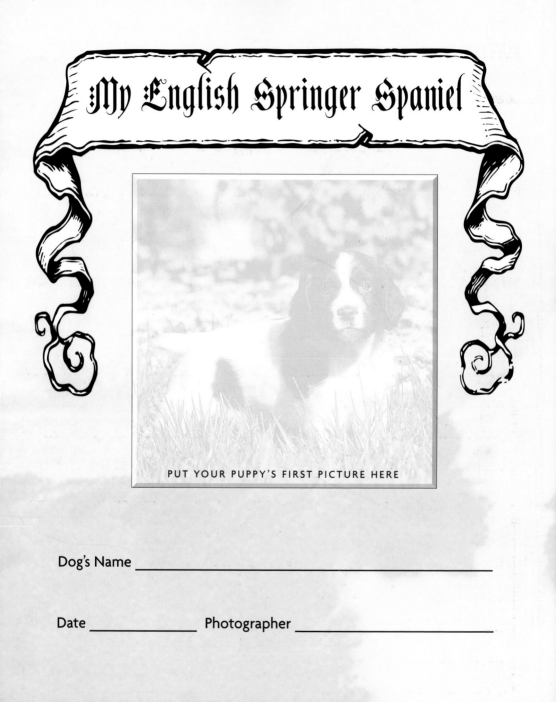

My English Springer Spaniel

PUT YOUR PUPPY'S FIRST PICTURE HERE

Dog's Name _____

Date _____ Photographer _____